DIGITIZED

Spiritual Implications of Technology

CONCORDIA PUBLISHING HOUSE · SAINT LOUIS

Dr. Bernard Bull

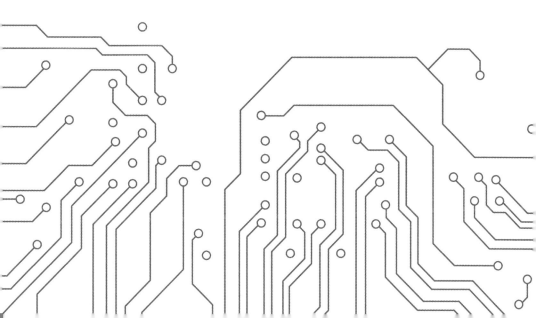

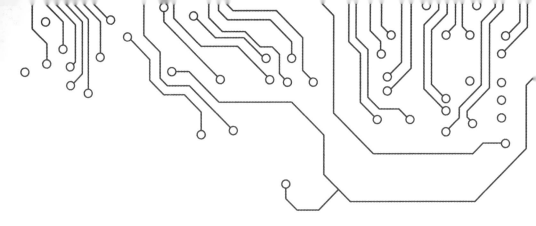

Copyright © 2018 Concordia Publishing House
3558 S. Jefferson Avenue, St. Louis, MO 63118-3968
1-800-325-3040 · www.cph.org

Scripture quotations are from the ESV® Bible (The Holy Bible, English Standard Version®), copyright © 2001 by Crossway, a publishing ministry of Good News Publishers. Used by permission. All rights reserved.

Catechism quotations are from *Luther's Small Catechism with Explanation,* copyright © 1986 Concordia Publishing House.

Quotations marked AE are from Luther's Works. American Edition. 75 vols. St. Louis: Concordia, and Philadelphia: Muhlenberg and Fortress, 1955– .

Manufactured in the United States of America

1 2 3 4 5 6 7 8 9 10   27 26 25 24 23 22 21 20 19 18

TABLE OF CONTENTS

Introduction

In 1997, I gave my first presentation at a professional conference, an educational technology conference in Chicago. The conference organizers scheduled my session for late in the morning on the first day, but I did not expect much interest in my topic. The organizers must have thought the same thing because they located my presentation in a small room on the second floor as far away from any other session as possible. There were enough chairs for about twenty-five people. You see, this was an educational technology conference, but the title of my presentation was "The Adverse Impact of Technology in Education."

Arriving early to get my computer set up with the projector, I prepared myself for a small group of attendees. I thought this would be a good opportunity to get comfortable with speaking at professional conferences, so I welcomed the idea of an intimate, low-key session. I think I brought only twenty copies of the handout. As I got my PowerPoint presentation ready and displayed on the screen, I reviewed my notes one last time and waited for people to arrive.

Fifteen minutes before the session was scheduled to begin, the room was a little more than half full. It calmed my nerves a bit to know I would be speaking in front of a small group. More people streamed into the room over the next fifteen minutes until all of the seats were full. But that did not stop people from coming into the room. They lined up along the sides and the back wall. Some sat on the floor near the front. Even more gathered outside the double-door entrance. By the time I was ready to start my presentation, I estimated that there were close to seventy people packed into that small room.

Why would so many people come to a session on the adverse impact of technology in education at a conference on educational technology, a conference that otherwise touted the grand benefits of using technology in schools? I still do not know the answer to that question, but something about the topic resonated with the people. I was not the only person concerned about the dangers and downsides of life and learning in an increasingly technological age.

In the years leading up to that presentation, I had become a fervent reader of anything written by educator and author Neil Postman. He wrote *Technopoly*,[1] *The End of Education*,[2] and many other books where he shared his critiques and concerns about our technology-shaped world and communities. From there, I immersed myself in the

---

1   Neil Postman, *Technopoly* (New York: Alfred A. Knopf, 1991).
2   Neil Postman, *The End of Education* (New York: Vintage Books, 1996).

works of a variety of other authors who added depth to my thinking about the role of media and technology in society: Jacques Ellul, Lewis Mumford, Marshall McLuhan, Walter Ong, and many others.[3] This reading challenged many of my assumptions about technology, and I developed a more nuanced and critical (but not necessarily negative) approach to studying the nature of life and learning in our technological age.

This was the body of work I drew upon for that presentation. I started the session by asking a question: Is technology neutral? Without expanding on the topic, I invited people to share their viewpoints, which launched a wonderfully engaging exchange. Then I used that exchange to launch into ten topics that I believed called for educators' careful consideration. I talked about how technology was changing our approach to writing, research, and collaboration. I presented some of the early research on how the brain is physically reshaped by technology and talked about how young people, especially those before age 5 or 6, have difficulty distinguishing between what is reality and what is on the screen. We discussed the potential health concerns caused by growing amounts of screen time.

> **Technology is one of those words we use often but rarely take time to define. Throughout this book, I will be using a broad definition of technology: "applied systematic or scientific knowledge." Using this definition, a technology can be anything from a computer to a pencil, a diet to a work schedule, email to advanced or complex software, a hammer to a robot. However, you will also notice that I sometimes use the word technologies, the plural. In those instances, I am referring to specific technologies or a collection of them. It is also helpful to note that I will put the greatest emphasis on digital technologies, those technologies that come to us through the many screens and digital devices in our lives.**

The group remained engaged throughout my one-hour presentation, and when it came time for questions and answers, at least ten or fifteen hands went up almost instantly. The first few questions came from what seemed like a line of grimacing software vendors standing in the back of the room. (My presentation was not an endorsement for their products, so they must have felt a need to defend themselves.) Others asked about practical implications for the classroom. Still others, even though this was a conference for teachers and school leaders, shared stories and concerns about the impact of technology on their own children.

---

3   Many of these authors are often associated with a newer field sometimes called "media ecology." For more information on this field and a myriad of writings, see the Media Ecology Association website at http://www.media-ecology.org.

In that presentation, I stated what I still consider to be sage advice to anyone reading this book. While much of it came from Neil Postman, I believe it is as valuable today as it was when he first started writing and talking about it in the 1990s. My advice goes something like this: I'm not suggesting that you stop using technology or that you choose to go the route of the Amish (although I have great respect for the Amish in regard to technology for reasons I will share later in this text). What I am suggesting is that there is more to technology than just learning how to use it. As Postman and many other media ecologists have explained, technology uses and shapes us as much as we use and shape it. I suggest that we take the time to think deeply about how technology works on us. What are the benefits? What are the limitations? What does a given technology make possible? What does it make less likely? These questions will help us become more conscious about the impact of technology in our lives and help us make conscious decisions about our use of it. I challenge us to better understand how technology uses us and to make more intentional choices concerning what we will do about it.

These questions form the basis and structure for this book. They represent the pursuit of the "examined life" in an increasingly digital age.[4] Technology is part of culture—it is a cultural artifact. So I argue that it is good, even essential, to better understand its place in our culture. Technology is increasingly integral in our homes, schools, libraries, grocery stores, communities, churches, places of work, government, hospitals and doctor's offices, and nearly every aspect of our modern world. We do not want to merely follow wherever the technologies lead us; so we are wise to recognize both their benefits and their limitations in order to live examined, thoughtful, alert, and deliberate lives. Therefore, as technology continuously changes almost everything about daily life, let us consider how it helps and hinders our relationships, spiritual lives, physical well-being, emotional lives, intellectual lives, leisure, work, and home lives.

Much of my professional work at Concordia University Wisconsin focuses upon following trends, especially in education. I track trends and develop methods to help people anticipate what is likely to stick and what is not, aiding them in creating plans and strategies for the future. I help people prepare for the future. This is not an exact science, and I get things wrong from time to time, but with the right tools and strategies,

---

4   Plato, *Plato—Five Dialogues: Euthyphro, Apology, Crito, Meno, Phaedo,* trans. Benjamin Jowett (New York: LG Classics, 2016), 38. While there is a more nuanced explanation of "the examined life" in this citation, my usage in this text is broader. By it, I am suggesting that we be more thoughtful and deliberate about the role of technology in our lives. There is value in careful and prayerful consideration about the role of technology. Without that, we can easily and unexpectedly be drawn away from some of our most precious beliefs and values.

some of this forecasting is not as difficult as some might think. It is time-consuming to be sure, but it does not require genius. Yet, when I speak about the emerging future, I often run into despairing individuals who feel like they are Dorothy in the *Wizard of Oz*. One moment they are in their home in Kansas, the next they are plopped into an entirely different and strange world and are wondering how that happened so quickly.

People often think that the technologies that now dominate our lives are overnight changes. They appeared suddenly one day. In no time, new technologies seem to be everywhere, reshaping some part of our lives. Yet, this is not how technologies are incorporated into society. Most develop over years, even decades. We often see hints of them. Some people embrace these technologies long before they become part of the mainstream; these people are known as "early adopters," a term coined by author Everett Rogers, a widely respected theorist and sociologist whose work focused on the sociology of communication technologies as well as the social aspects of leading innovations.[5] Early iterations and versions of technologies are piloted and experimented with in segments of the population before they are found in the average household, school, pocket, or purse.

Do not get me wrong. Technology *is* moving incredibly fast, and it *is* hard to keep up with the changes, even for those of us whose work it is to follow such trends. Yet, the changes do not occur as suddenly as they appear to. They catch us off guard because we do not acknowledge them or think about them until after they have become the new normal. When we welcome a new technology into our lives, we may let it play out as a novelty. We often do not think about how far-reaching it might be, how it will affect us, and what we will do about it. Yet, I believe it is important for us to change this. If we want to take responsibility, to have a voice and a choice about what happens to us, our loved ones, our families, our communities, our places of worship, and our schools, then we must take on this responsibility whole-heartedly. It is time to cultivate the habit of thinking deeply and often about the technologies in our world and our lives. This will assist us in making wise choices not only about the technologies we currently have and use, but also in areas where we have less choice about the technologies we encounter. In those instances, the intentional, deliberate approach to using technology at least increases our awareness of the benefits, limitations, and implications of our technologies. That being said, I suspect there is a common misconception about technology that prevents us from doing this.

---

5   Everett M. Rogers, *Diffusion of Innovations,* 5th ed., (New York: Free Press, 2005), 22.

JUST A TOOL?

"Technology is just a tool," we think. "What good or ill comes from a given technology all depends upon how you use it." That is a common sentiment today, but it is also a fallacy. Technology is far from neutral. It has vast implications for our individual lives, families, communities, churches, schools, governments, and workplaces. It helps to shape how we think, speak, and act. While I appreciate the sentiment that everything depends upon our use of technology, since it is a tool, this mind-set has significant flaws and prevents us from exerting greater control over the role of technology in our lives.

It is helpful to begin by looking at a couple of definitions. According to the Merriam-Webster dictionary, a *technology* is "the practical application of knowledge especially in a particular area."[6] By this definition, a technology is designed to carry out a specific function. It is not neutral because it has an intended use, and it is not especially helpful for other uses. If I have a hammer, it's quite useful in driving in a nail to connect two pieces of wood. It is far less helpful if I use it to comb my hair. That is because the technology of the hammer has the specific function of hitting things, not removing knots from my hair. Someone designed it with certain purposes in mind and not others. By its very nature, a hammer has a fundamental bias.

This is what I mean when I say that technology is not a neutral tool. When I use the hammer example, this fact seems apparent; but what about when I mention a modern technology such as the cell phone, which is actually a collection of hundreds of technologies? These modern and multifaceted technologies have biases that are not as easily clarified or well understood. It takes time, study, and reflection for understanding to surface.

The Oxford Living Dictionary defines *technology* as "an applied scientific knowledge,"[7] though some prefer "systematic" to "scientific." Regardless, this definition broadens our thinking beyond hardware and devices and challenges us to consider that technologies can be ideas, models, methods, strategies, frameworks, and other abstract creations. A diet plan, in this sense, is a technology. So are time-management approaches, school grading systems, books, and traffic laws, which are established to promote road safety.

In each of these examples, my statement about technologies not being neutral stands. A collection of laws to govern traffic has biases. It amplifies some things and

---

6   "Technology," *Merriam-Webster Online*, https://www.merriam-webster.com/dictionary/technology (accessed August 9, 2017).

7   "Technology," *Oxford Living Dictionaries*, https://en.oxforddictionaries.com/definition/technology (accessed August 9, 2017).

muffles others. It rewards careful, cautious driving and orderliness. It favors collective good over individual good. At the same time, it might delay you in reaching your destination or inhibit other individual goals.

It is important to keep in mind that I am not claiming that technology is good or bad or has some sort of integrated moral agenda. Rather, I look at technology with what I call affordances and limitations. Each technology makes certain things more possible, more likely—it has affordances. Each technology also makes other things less possible or less likely—it has limitations.

AVOIDING THE TRAP

There is a persistent risk, when addressing a topic like technology, of falling into the trap of legalism—of turning cultural or personal preferences into law. We risk believing that our subjective viewpoints are aligned with the timeless and unchanging objective truth of God's Word. In a spirit of helpfulness and in the pursuit of something clear, understandable, and practical, we create new commandments for ourselves that we then place on the shoulders of others as well. We establish "top ten" lists of what Christians parents should or should not require of their children when it comes to cell phone or Internet usage. We establish moral standards about the amount of television consumption that is appropriate for us or others. We judge ourselves and others on the basis of any number of similar man-made rules. Such lists and rules can certainly be useful in our individual lives, families, and communities; but we must be incredibly careful that we do not treat them or act as if they were commandments or standards from God. I hope and pray that I have not fallen into that trap in this book. It is my sincere effort to approach this topic with humility and to rely on God's Word to help us navigate life in this connected and digital age.

I do not spoon-feed answers to the dilemmas of our age here. I simply juxtapose the dilemmas and God's Word and invite the reader to grapple with the application of God's Word to these new and ever-changing circumstances. I have too high of a regard for objective truth to believe that my subjective viewpoints are absolutes for the rest of the world. That has the dual risk of placing man-made moral burdens on others while diminishing the value and importance of the actual absolute truths revealed in the Scriptures.

Those expecting simple and straightforward commandments for the digital age will be disappointed in this book because we do not need more Commandments. The Ten Commandments are our guide in all matters, just as they were when God first gave them to Moses. The context of our daily lives is different from the wilderness that the children of Israel wandered through, of course. Nevertheless, throughout this book, I invite the reader to apply God's Word to current life, thought, trends, and events. I will, at times, share my viewpoint, but my desire is to do it in a way that clearly distinguishes between opinion and timeless truth.

SO, WHY THIS BOOK?

This is a book for Christians who are seeking wisdom in navigating the intersection of faith and life in the digital age. We know that "the fear of the LORD is instruction in wisdom, and humility comes before honor" (Proverbs 15:33). We also learn from the Book of James, "If any of you lacks wisdom, let him ask God, who gives generously to all without reproach, and it will be given him" (1:5). These verses prepare us to approach this topic with humility and to recognize our flaws and limitations while also recognizing God's supreme wisdom and love for us in Jesus Christ. We humbly examine life in this connected age with our Bibles open and our minds and hearts receptive to what God will teach us. We turn to God in repentance, trusting in the atoning sacrifice of Jesus Christ. We humbly pray for the wisdom about which James speaks, doing so with confidence that our loving and just heavenly Father will indeed hear and answer these prayers.

HOW TO USE THIS BOOK

This book, then, is a technology in itself—one that brings with it both affordances and limitations. You have decisions about how you will use this technology. You might choose to read it alone, reflecting and prayerfully considering its content. You might be reading it as a required text for a course or for a group study at your church. Those contexts bring with them a chance to engage in the good work of "iron sharpen[ing] iron" (Proverbs 27:17) as you discuss, challenge, question, and learn alongside one another. You might also be reading this book as part of a book club, over coffee or some other beverage, gathering to discuss what you are learning and thinking. That is a wonderful way to read, reflect on, and consider the implications of a book. You might even be reading this book with others from different parts of the country or world, gathering in an online community or connecting via social media. Those medias offer you a different type of conversation community by using the technologies.

Any of these contexts are possibilities for how you may use this book. I personally am fond of finding a way to think and talk about the contents of a good book with other people, learning in community. In fact, I wrote this book with that particular usage in mind. Navigating faith and life in a digital age is something done most effectively in families and in Christian congregations and communities. We gather together, challenge and sharpen one another, encourage one another, learn from one another, study the Scriptures together, and join in prayer. It is my hope and prayer, therefore, that the majority of people will read and use this book within families, congregations, and Christian classrooms as a launch pad into careful and prayerful personal study and consideration.

SCOPE OF THE BOOK

As I define it, *technology* is an incredibly broad term. There are many topics I mention in this book but do not explore in depth. Instead, I opted to devote the greatest attention to communication technologies and technologies that offer us diverse media and information. I did this because such technologies are some of the most prevalent in our daily lives. For many Americans, such technologies garner attention for many hours each day. Therefore, I deemed these to be good and important places to start our consideration about the spiritual implications of technology in modern life.

BE A BEREAN

Regardless of the context in which you will grapple with and make sense of the ideas in this book, I suggest you do so with the mind-set of a Berean. We read about the Bereans in the Book of Acts: "Now these Jews were more noble than those in Thessalonica; they received the word with all eagerness, examining the Scriptures daily to see if these things were so" (17:11). The Bereans did not blindly accept and follow Paul and his words. They examined and analyzed. They compared what he taught with the Scriptures. I invite you to approach this book with that same method: analyzing and testing what you read here with what you read in the Bible. There are plenty of topics for which we have no direct and prescriptive teaching from God's Word, but that does not mean God is silent on these issues. The Holy Spirit works through the Word "for teaching, for reproof, for correction, and for training in righteousness, that the man of God may be complete, equipped for every good work" (2 Timothy 3:16–17). I am grateful that you have chosen to devote time to reading this book and considering the implications of modern technology on your faith and life. I trust you will do so with your Bible open, testing what I write against the ultimate norm and source of doctrine for the Christian.

There are two parts in this book. The first examines attributes and experiences of living in the digital world. You will be encouraged to describe and reflect on how digital culture is changing how people think, act, and work. We will consider the influence of technology upon our beliefs and values. Because new technologies are introduced almost daily, this first section is far from an exhaustive list, but I include some of the more prevalent aspects of modern life. Use this first section to think about the impact of these various attributes on your life, for your family, and in your church, community, and workplace.

Following the thirteen chapters on features of life in a digital age, part 2 offers insights and suggestions for how we might want to engage individually, as a family, and as a church with these (and other) attributes. Again, this is not exhaustive or a defined how-to list; rather, it is intended as a starting point for your prayerful reflection and discussion.

In the end, my goal for this book is simple: that it would help you consider the challenges and opportunities of being a Christian in a digitized age.

PART 1

HOW IS TECHNOLOGY SHAPING US?

In this section, we look at thirteen aspects of technology and how it affects our lives and influences beliefs and values. While there is some commentary about the implications of these influences and what we can do about them, most of that discussion is reserved for the second section of the book. As you read this section, consider how you have experienced or witnessed these influences. How do you see them at work in your life, family, church, workplace, and community?

HOW DO YOU FIND GOOD INFORMATION?

When you are trying to find good or accurate information (maybe both), how do you go about it? Do you settle for what shows up on your first Internet search? Do you ask friends, colleagues, or family for suggestions? Do you turn to a few trusted and credible sources to guide your decisions? Consider recording some of your answers to these questions. What are some of the benefits or limitations to your most common approaches to finding information?

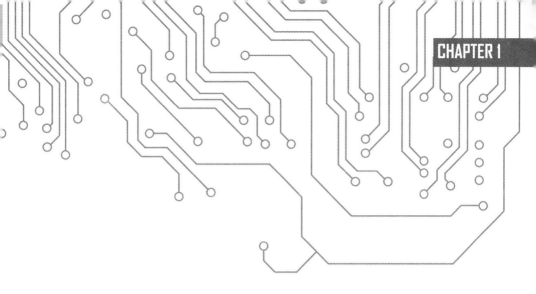

CHAPTER 1

Information Overload and Information Addiction

Neil Postman explains the cult of information in which we find ourselves this way:

> There is information. There is knowledge. And there is wisdom. Information consists of small bits: ones and zeros, letters, numbers, words, individual and discrete facts. Knowledge is more than that. It pulls information together into a cohesive structure; it implies understanding and meaning from information. Wisdom, on the other hand, consists of discernment and judgement.[8]

Wisdom is the ability to determine that which is good, true, right, and prudent. In Philippians 4:8, Paul writes, "Finally, brothers, whatever is true, whatever is honorable, whatever is just, whatever is pure, whatever is lovely, whatever is commendable, if there is any excellence, if there is anything worthy of praise, think about such things." This is a call to wisdom, not just simple information or knowledge.

The late journalist Miles Kington is credited with saying, "*Knowledge* is knowing that a tomato is a fruit. *Wisdom* is knowing not to put it in a fruit salad." This distinction between information, knowledge, and wisdom is important to the Christian tradition. As we read in Proverbs 4:6–7, "Do not forsake her [wisdom], and she will keep you; love her, and she will guard you. The beginning of wisdom is this: Get wisdom, and whatever you get, get insight." Scripture tells us to value wisdom and to give it priority in our lives.

---

8   Neil Postman, "Informing Ourselves to Death," Internet Archive, October 11, 1990, https://web.archive.org/web/20090107102853/http://world.std.com/~jimf/informing.html (accessed March 19, 2017).

Postman continued with commentary on our current age, in which the average person has access to more information than ever before in history. We are just a click (or a question, if we ask Siri or Alexa) away from information about almost any topic. While not disregarding the benefit of information, Postman makes an important claim:

> While we have so much information available to us today, information does not solve many of our greatest problems in life. Those problems call for wisdom. Our world might have a fascination with information, but the simple accumulation of information is not enough.[9]

It is easy to forget this. If we want to explore a topic, we can collect countless links, articles, and videos. In fact, sometimes we are so caught up collecting the information that we do not fully absorb, analyze, and understand what we gather. We lose sight of the goal—which is not to compile as much information as possible, but to increase our knowledge and, ultimately, develop wisdom.

Information addiction, while not a clinical condition, is easy to fall into. Have you ever started working on a home project by browsing the web for images, examples, and ideas? It is not uncommon to find ourselves spending countless hours browsing and collecting ideas and images, even to the point that it takes up more time than the project itself. Before we know it, the information collection takes away from time that we could have spent on the actual project.

Here's another familiar example: anyone with a physical symptom can search the Internet for information about it. There are countless medical websites and online medical dictionaries we can browse to self-diagnose. There are instances where people use this information with a good outcome. They may learn about treatment options, clinical trials, or support groups. Yet, there are also many instances of people working themselves into high levels of anxiety because of the information they find. Without the wisdom of a trained medical person to discern what information is relevant and what is not, a person can easily become distraught, thinking the Internet is telling them that the rash on their arm could be evidence of a rare, exotic, life-threatening parasitic infestation or worse. Or it could be the first time they discover they're allergic to poison ivy.

The reality is that while we have access to information, we may not have the formal training, in-depth knowledge, or wisdom that allows us to correctly discern the information at our fingertips. Amid information overload, we can forget that having access to information is not the same as having expertise. We may assume, for example, that having access to the information makes knowledge acquisition and the cultivation of

---

9   Ibid.

wisdom unnecessary. Why spend so much time learning something when we can just look it up when the need arises?

Of course, it does not take much to challenge such a notion. If I am a surgeon, is it adequate for me to not prepare for a surgery, to assume I can just search for a helpful YouTube video whenever I need to perform a procedure on a patient? We reject such an example as absurd, yet the temptation to devalue the role of expertise, competence, and wisdom remains quite prevalent in society.

Conversely, ready access to information changes the way we think about education. That is, some information is not as important to memorize as it once was. I hesitate to give specific examples as I find that many people have a special commitment to the idea of memorizing certain facts. However, I encourage readers to pause and reflect on what they still consider important to memorize and what they do not. As one example, I personally contend that memorizing a long list of phone numbers is far less relevant for me today, given that I have them all in the contact list on my mobile phone. I still remember a short list of critical numbers, for emergencies when devices are not readily available, but beyond that, memorizing phone numbers is less important to me.

What is important is that we do not assume that memorization or true learning is no longer necessary in all domains and contexts. There is still need for hard work to cultivate knowledge and skill over an extended period. Learning is more than information acquisition; it includes personal development and formation that do not happen by simply accessing information.

In a world of potential information overload and even information addiction, the need arises to develop a more robust understanding and appreciation of the role of wisdom. One of the ways wisdom is acquired concerning a topic or skill is through the arduous and often unglamorous process of developing expertise and competence.

We are in an era shaped by data mining, informatics, big data analysis, and data analytics. We track a multitude of human behaviors—and this is not a neutral activity. The collection and analysis of data about individuals has ethical considerations. If and how we collect and analyze the data about people in our churches, schools, and communities, for example, is not a straightforward exercise. If you ask people in organizations why they are collecting data, you will likely receive many reasonable answers. You may also find some that strike you as concerning. Decisions about data collection call for wisdom and prayerful consideration because they often have complex implications. The purpose of the data collection might be for a good cause or reason, but there are also considerations about privacy; the danger of compromised information; or issues around how people might misuse or misinterpret some of the data, especially when it is taken out of context.

The scope and impact of data collection is not new to our era. Humankind has a long history of seeking to quantify things that are not inclined toward quantification. Consider your favorite song, novel, or piece of art. Would you agree that a careful quantitative analysis of it would give an accurate picture of why it is your favorite? Would you be satisfied with a quantitative analysis or a compilation of descriptive data in place of the real thing? Suppose you went to an art museum and discovered that every painting and sculpture had been replaced with a chart, a diagram, or spreadsheet. Of course, we realize that there is a difference between statistics on something and the real thing.

Nonetheless, we live in an age of quantification. What we can measure and quantify garners more attention than what we cannot. Consider how this drives debates in the modern education system. Some lobby for standardized tests that allow us to quantify the intelligence, aptitude, or mastery of a learner. Yet, as Christians, we know that education is not about achieving a certain test score as much as it is growing in mind, body, and spirit. We know that it is difficult or impossible to rate and rank some of the most important aspects of learning. It is about growing in ways that allow us to love our neighbor, to live out our current and future callings. In other words, education is about cultivating wisdom.

COGNITIVE OVERLOAD

In the field of psychology, there is a concept known as "cognitive load theory" that is relevant to this topic. Cognitive load theorists focus upon the effort required to pay attention to or understand something. It is a theory used to guide people who design educational resources and learning experiences to increase opportunities for student learning. The general concept is that learning is hindered or enhanced by the way content is presented.

Consider the example that emerged in some schools when interactive whiteboards (called by the brand name SMART Board) were installed in classrooms. These devices function like whiteboards of the past, but they include computer projection and are touch-sensitive. Teachers or students can project documents and web pages, write on the board, and interact with computer-generated visuals. The use of such a technology in classrooms increases student engagement and learning.

Yet, that is not always what happens, especially when interactive whiteboards are used in math classrooms. Imagine this scenario: A student comes into the room for math class, sits at her desk, takes out her book, and opens her notebook, ready to take notes. The teacher is standing in the front of the room at the interactive whiteboard, which is flanked by traditional whiteboards. As the teacher takes the class through the lesson, she moves between the traditional and the interactive whiteboards. The students are expected to pay attention to the textbook, the notebook, the interactive whiteboard, the traditional whiteboard, and the teacher. This shifting of attention increases the students' mental load. This is less of a challenge for students who know the subject well, but those who struggle to understand the concepts are distracted by the variety of focal points and have less comprehension. They will experience cognitive overload.

This is not unlike what some people experience when they attend worship services that require them to look at words on a projection screen upfront, on the pages of a hymnal, and in a bulletin. This is less challenging for people who know the order of service and format. But it will create cognitive overload and decreased processing capacity for those who don't.

Now consider the daily bombardment of information from countless sources. Despite the deluge, we find ourselves craving even more information, so we deliberately seek it via our devices. That craving may not be beneficial when it comes to attention span and depth of understanding. We may be distracted, confused, forget facts that were previously easy to remember. As Nicholas Carr explains in *The Shallows*, we experience overload when we take in more information than we are capable of processing.[10]

Information overload does not contribute to deep thinking, critical thinking skills, or the cultivation of wisdom. It promotes knee-jerk reactions and quick decisions as coping mechanisms. We may even shut down emotionally (which could explain those blank expressions when people are absorbed in browsing the web). Carr suggests this is an induced numbness caused by overwhelming ourselves with too much information.[11]

WISDOM

Consider another scenario. Imagine you have the task of finding the answer to an important and complex question at work. Your supervisor places you in a large room full of thousands of books and stacks of paper journals and whitepapers. It would take hundreds of years to read everything in the room, yet you have to find the answer in this sea of information. Where do you start? What strategy do you use to accomplish what feels like an impossible task? Do you go with the book that's closest to you, or do

10   Nicholas G. Carr, *The Shallows: What the Internet is Doing to our Brains* (New York: Norton, 2011), 125–29.

11   Ibid., 209–10.

you browse the stacks and piles, looking for something that relates? Do you start with what is on the top of the piles or the bottom?

Now, let us adjust the scenario. You are in that same room, but all the books and journals are gone. Instead, you are sitting at a computer with the Google homepage open. You type in your question, and more than a million matching responses pop up. Where do you begin? Do you just go with that which showed up first? How many pages do you scan? When you find an answer, do you test it against more sources? How much scanning and reading is enough?

For those who have more nuanced skills in information literacy, this is a manageable task. They have developed systems, strategies, and methods to work through information challenges. For others, the volume of data is overwhelming and could even lead to anxiety or abandoning the task altogether. Still others use a strategy or method they like but that might not be helpful in finding the right or best answer. They go to their favorite sites, disregarding unfamiliar ones. They look only at what is easily accessible in full text online, while the best answers may be in new articles that are currently available only in print. They limit their search to the first page or two of the search results or they limit the key words used in their search.

As we will continue to explore, the nature of information and news in the digital world is of no small importance for the Christian because truth is central to our worldview. Furthermore, many of the moral and religious messages that the average person will encounter today will come through digital media. They come from a wild blend of social media, news sites, and entertainment outlets. As we are increasingly immersed in this vast ocean of information, we must remember that not all of it is true, nor does it point us to the ultimate source of truth. Let us continue this in the next chapter as we focus our attention on news in the digital age.

DISCUSSION AND REFLECTION QUESTIONS

- Do you find yourself seeking wisdom versus information? What do you observe in regard to this in schools, the community, and the workplace?

- Can you think of times when information overload or the accumulation of information distracted you or others from more important priorities?

- The church is in a unique position given its fundamental value of wisdom over just information. How might our churches more actively point people in our communities to the value of wisdom versus information?

WHAT DO YOU MODEL?

As illustrated in this next chapter, children are not the only ones spending hours each day in front of screens. Parents and other adults are doing the same thing. Parents and children might be looking at, watching, listening to, or interacting with technology in different ways, but screens are ubiquitous. In such a digitized world, it can become easy to let the draw of the screen take us away from the rich opportunities for conversation and community with the people around us: family members, friends, neighbors, and others. What strategies do you use or might you use to make sure the people around you know that you value them and time with them, even in such a screen-driven age?

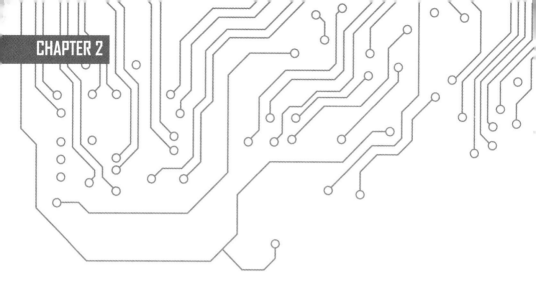

CHAPTER 2

"Cat's in the Cradle" Goes Digital

In 1974, Harry Chapin released the song "Cat's in the Cradle," a moving ballad about the relationship between a father and his son. Early in the song, the father announces the birth of his son while he is away on business. As the song continues, the boy grows up, admires his father, and seeks to be like him. Yet, he craves time with his father, asking to do things like play ball. The dad explains that he can't because he has too much work to do. Instead of becoming sad, the boy walks away with the resolve to be like his father one day. The song continues in the same way until the end, when the son is grown and the father, an old man, yearns to spend quality time with his son. Yet, the son is too busy. He became just like his father, just as he always wanted to.[12]

This song remains a warning to parents around the world to enjoy time with their children and to recognize that they are the model for their children. Yet modern life often values that which happens outside of the home more than what happens inside the home. Modern society and its technological innovations create so many ways to accommodate longer work days and to focus on getting ahead in our careers that we fail to enjoy the God-given gift of family and neglect to take the time to enjoy one another.

We sometimes forget that relationships are not a means to an end. Soon after creation, before sin entered the world, God said, "It is not good that the man should be alone" (Genesis 2:18). God is a God of relationship, and He created us as relational beings. Put another way, God created us to be in relationship with Himself and with one another. That is a core part of who we are—our purpose and identity—and family is a core expression of our relatedness. "We love because He first loved us" (1 John 4:19).

---

12   Harry Chapin, "Cat's in the Cradle," *Verities & Balderdash*, Connecticut Recording Studios, 1974, compact disc.

The "Cat's in the Cradle" warning applies even more today. Only now, there is another dimension to it. Instead of picturing Dad heading out on a jet plane to some distant meeting, we can see Dad or Mom being just as distant from his or her family while being in the same room. The equivalent distance today is a parent immersed in a screen: on the cell phone playing a game or texting someone, or on a tablet distracted by a favorite show as an escape from a long and stressful day at work.

I am not arguing that any of these activities is morally wrong. I am simply pointing out a need for balance. Parents have to go to work, engage in work over the phone, or work online over the weekend. That can and does happen for many of us. Parents also can enjoy a good television show or a digital chat with a friend.

However, it is wise for us to remember that we are setting an example for our children. Like the boy in the song, our children may well be saying (verbally or not) that they want to be just like us when they grow up. What is interesting is that parents of the 1980s and 1990s often expressed concern that their children were glued to a screen, playing video games for countless hours instead of getting outside and playing. Those children are now today's parents, and they have continued this high frequency of screen time. In fact, these parents are modeling life on the screen for their own kids.

Of course, this is not limited to parents. Almost all of us have choices about the extent to which we attend to the people in our physical proximities compared to the other distractions in our immediate surroundings. This is a choice we face daily, but our phones and tablets create options that did not exist in past generations. They present new cries for our attention.

When I speak at a conference, I realize that the people have far more complex choices in front of them than simply staying in my session or going to another or hitting the golf course. Now, people are capable of attending to multiple resources at the same time. They might choose to stay in my session and listen part of the time while also reading and replying to emails, texting a friend or family member, and scanning the web for the best local restaurants in anticipation of dinner.

When I am standing in line at the grocery store, I have the choice between paying attention to my surroundings and the people in line with me or catching up on what is happening with my friends via my favorite social media app. This is not new to anyone reading this book. It is daily life in an increasingly digital and connected world.

When speaking at a pastor's conference about this topic a few years ago, one pastor told me a story about providing marital counseling. At the heart of the couple's challenges, he discerned, was a sort of avoidance of each other, an unwillingness to speak directly and candidly to each other. When they shared their challenges with him, the pastor asked if the two of them ever talked to each other about these things, just the two of them. "Sort of," one of them explained. It turns out that they would sit in the same room, but not next to each other. Or one might be in the kitchen and the other in the dining room. Then they would argue back and forth on their phones via text. Even though they were mere feet from each other, they did not sit next to the other and look each other in the eyes, much less talk through their challenges face-to-face.

Have you ever observed a couple out for dinner at a nice restaurant? The food is out of this world, and the ambience is ideal for a romantic date. Yet both people at the table are staring down at their phones instead of talking to each other.

Again, I do not share these stories to cast judgment, but to inspire consideration of the demands for our attention in this world. It is no longer taken for granted that we will give our full attention to other people in the same room as us. Many things are calling for our attention, and our devices connect us to those many things.

As a manager, I have come to realize this challenge while having weekly meetings with my team. These meetings are fifteen minutes a week, a brief check-in. But for some reason, I continually find myself drawn during those fifteen minutes to check my texts or emails as soon as my phone buzzes. That is until one year, on an anonymous evaluation, a person gently shared this concern: "Sometimes it seems like you are too busy for me." That is the last thing I meant to communicate through my actions. I want to be available for the people on my team. I want them to know I care about them and that they are worth far more than fifteen minutes of undivided attention. Yet, without consciously thinking about it, I allowed the demand of the device to divert me from being present in the moment and communicating that I value the other person.

How do we learn to make wise choices among the expanding options? As we read in the previous chapter, tools and technologies like the cell phone are not neutral. The cell phone has core values of immediacy and connectivity across space; it asks for our attention *now*. Giving attention to the person directly in front of us is no longer the primary choice, and most of us can point to experiences when this choice has occurred in our lives.

I can be in an important one-on-one meeting with a colleague at work and find myself almost involuntarily pulling out my phone and glancing at it. In fact, because I use my phone for several tasks (to send email, for one), sometimes it becomes a third member of the meeting. We connect with resources and people in the moment to work through an important problem or question. Other times the phone simply calls out to us, sometimes literally, reminding us that others seek our attention at that moment as well. For some of us, every moment involves multiple demands for our attention, and we must choose who or what we value in that moment.

Have you been in a conversation with someone when his or her phone rings? They look down at the phone, apologize but explain that they really need to answer this call. Important phone calls certainly happened in the past as well, but now every call is potentially important. Even the fact that we are compelled to look at our phone changes the nature of our conversations and interactions.

Please note that I am not suggesting we establish rules that we impose on others and ourselves (though rules of etiquette are negotiated in every context). Yet, these moments are prime opportunities for us to think about our beliefs and values and how we will live out these beliefs and values in the presence of these technologies and the demands they make on our attention. If we do not reflect and make conscious decisions, the technologies will likely make the decisions for us.

This truth applies to all aspects of our lives, of course. If technology truly is values-laden, then which values become amplified or muzzled at any given moment? We can ask this about technology's place in our homes, workplaces, communities, churches, and elsewhere. With this in mind, let us return to the song "Cat's in the Cradle."

In the song, the dad did not formally decide one day that he would prioritize working and getting ahead in his career over spending quality time with his son. The point of the song, I believe, is that he let the tyranny of the urgent take over. For us in the digital age, this is even more likely. Our cell phones connect us to our work twenty-four hours a day, seven days a week. There are emails to answer during dinner, in the evening, on weekends and holidays, and when we are playing catch with our kids in the backyard. Text messages and voicemails demand our attention. Most of us do not consciously say, "I value this email more than the person in front of me." Unless we are a transplant surgeon or a firefighter, we do not announce, "This pressing issue at work is more significant than the need to be fully present with my family or friend at this moment." In fact, that email we receive at home does not always carry such priority. Yet, sometimes we treat it that way and let it hijack our deliberate consideration and decisions.

What I am offering is an opportunity for us to think deeply about life and learning in the digital age. This is an opportunity to be more prayerful and deliberate in our decisions about the role of technology in various areas of our lives. It is a chance to think about the beliefs and values that we hold most dear and to make technology decisions that affirm those beliefs and values. This is not just about criticizing the potential negative impact of technology. It is also about discovering ways in which it can be a blessing or benefit to us and others.

In Mark 12, we learn about the scribe who approached Jesus with a question:

> "Which commandment is the most important of all?" Jesus answered, "The most important is, 'Hear, O Israel: The Lord our God, the Lord is one. And you shall love the Lord your God with all your heart and with all your soul and with all your mind and with all your strength.' The second is this: 'You shall love your neighbor as yourself.'" (vv. 28–31)

In light of this, there is a fundamental question we need to ask about the role of technology in our lives—specifically, how does it serve as a tool to love God and our neighbors? As Christians, we are reminded by Martin Luther that we are "perfectly free lord of all, subject to none" and, at the same time, "perfectly dutiful servant of all, subject to all."[13] How does our use of technology fit into living out such truths?

Years ago, I had the opportunity to study and learn a little bit about Amish culture. For a long time, I had thought of the Amish as a people who were anti-technology. Yet, when I started reading about them, I realized that this was a flawed view. The Amish are not anti-technology as much as they are pro-community. In other words, they place a high value on their communities and way of life in their homes and communities, and they make decisions about technology use that amplify their values. Now you can certainly disagree with their lifestyle choices and how it effectively removes them from engaging with much of the world. We can also disagree with some of their theology. Yet the one thing I appreciate is the Amish recognition that technology is not neutral, that it influences the way we live in relationship to others, and that it is wise to prayerfully consider its role. Again, I offer a word of caution: it is easy to fall into the trap of legalism or antinomianism.

The fact is that God's love for us, expressed in the sacrifice of His only Son on our behalf, is something that is secure. His love and grace do not depend upon our getting this technology thing right. This is a fundamental truth I invite you to remember as we move forward. You are free in Christ. And knowing this truth, I invite you to consider how you will use that freedom to love your neighbors (including your most immediate neighbors—your family and the people you see every day) and how technology's role in your life will help or hinder that effort.

---

13 AE 31:344.

DISCUSSION AND REFLECTION QUESTIONS

- In the "Cat's in the Cradle" example in this chapter, we considered how the concerns are reversed. Today, the challenge is not just children on the screen, but also parents. How do you see technology changing the way in which parents and children interact today?

- What beliefs and values currently shape your decisions about what technologies you use and how you use them?

- A recurring theme in this book is how Jesus' command for us to love our neighbor relates to our use of technology. How do you see your current use of technology helping or hindering the love of your neighbor in different areas of your life?

HOW ARE THE TOOLS BUILDING YOU?

Some of the ideas in this chapter might seem abstract at first. Tools build us? Yet, try creating a list of two to four new technologies that you have added to your life in the last few years. Perhaps it is a fitness tracker like the Fitbit, a GPS, an online game you enjoy, a subscription to a video service like Hulu or Netflix, or any number of mobile phone apps. Take a moment to write down how your life was different before you started using the technology. What changed? See if you can identify ways in which that technology shaped you, your beliefs, your use of time, or something else. To what extent do you consider this a positive or negative change? How much did you notice that it was changing you?

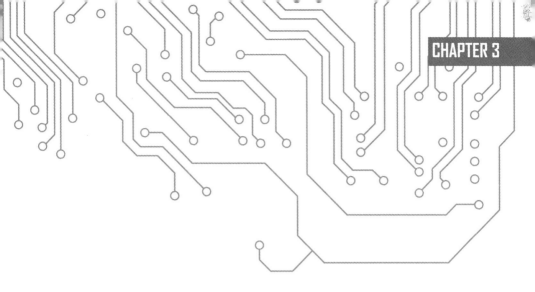

CHAPTER 3

We Build the Tools, and Then They Build Us

As John Culkin explained in his article about the ideas and influence of the media ecologist Marshall McLuhan, we begin by creating the technologies or tools, but after the technologies are implemented, these same creations begin to create or re-create us.[14] This is an important concept about life in a technological world. In chapter one, I made the case that technology is values-laden; it is not neutral. Then, in chapter two, I illustrated that this fact is important because it has an influence on our relationships and communities. In this chapter, I want to unpack McLuhan's concept that technologies shape us as we better understand the ways many current technologies are already shaping our values, our perception of the world, and more.

One of the more helpful books on this subject written in the last decade is Sherry Turkle's *Alone Together: How We Expect More from Technology and Less from One Another*.[15] Turkle has a three-decade history of grappling with social and psychological implications of technology in modern life, having written groundbreaking works about life online and the impact of the Internet on our notion of self.[16]

In *Alone Together*, Turkle writes about a growing concern regarding technology today: technology begins to expect and demand things from us. Along the way, people come to value and prefer interactions with technologies more than interactions

---

14 John Culkin, "A Schoolman's Guide to Marshall McLuhan," *Saturday Review*, March 18, 1967, 71–72.

15 Sherry Turkle, *Alone Together: Why We Expect More from Technology and Less from Each Other* (New York: Basic Books, 2013).

16 See Sherry Turkle, *Life on the Screen: Identity in the Age of the Internet* (New York: Touchstone, 1995) and *The Second Self: Computers and the Human Spirit* (New York: Simon & Schuster, 1984) for more on this topic.

with people. She argues that this creates a dangerous combination.[17] We start to expect things from technology that we previously expected from other humans. We seek comfort, encouragement, affirmation, knowledge, and even a sense of worth in and through the technologies in our lives today. She further explains that many people are attracted to connections that are readily available and ask little of us; even though they are demanding of our attention, the social or emotional risk is low. We often come to value the convenience of a connection more than the depth or authenticity of it.[18]

Some of you have witnessed the ways in which young people seek to build relationships with virtual assistants on their mobile devices. Siri, Cortana, and Alexa are not just playful ways to seek information in an audio format for some children. I have witnessed deeply personal "conversations." This is not new in some ways, as some people in the 1980s described leaving the television on in their homes for "company."

However, Turkle contends that phenomena such as relationships with virtual assistants and many other similar changes are leading up to what she calls the "robotic moment."[19] Movies like *The Terminator*, *Transformers*, or *Ex Machina* describe the robotic moment as the time when robots or machines exceed our human intelligence or capabilities and potentially take over our planet. This is not how Turkle looks at it. Instead, she sees the robotic moment as that time in history when people start preferring the technological to the human version of something. A child would rather play with a robot friend instead of a real human friend. The shut-in at church prefers (does not just settle for) a virtual church service over the intimacy of physically gathering in a space with other people and experiencing worship together. We prefer the safety of the technological solution to a human need or desire over the uncertainty and messiness of the human interaction.[20]

In fact, this idea of a robotic moment is not just confined to a single moment; this shift has been in progress for hundreds, if not thousands, of years. When mass-produced books arrived, some people began to prefer reading a book privately instead of listening to a book read to a large group. We started to prefer technological and automated services in our work and home that remove the need to interact with a human. A growing number of grocery and retail stores give us the option of self-checkout or even of having whatever is lacking in our cupboards shipped directly to us at the click of a button. There is no need to talk to a real person when we purchase something.

---

17   Turkle, *Alone Together*, 295.
18   Ibid.
19   Ibid., 9–10.
20   Ibid., 1.

Commerce is a technological exchange, and some have come to value the efficiency of that more than an interaction with a person. We do not need to talk to a bank teller to withdraw money. We just use our debit card at an ATM (which stands for automated teller machine, a name that even reflects how technology has replaced an interaction with a real person). So, as the preference for a technological rather than human option continues to expand, perhaps there is not a single robotic "moment" as Turkle explains it as much as a series of small robotic moments.

Could there be a time when people seek a technological solution to God's statement, "It is not good that the man should be alone"? This may seem far-fetched to some readers, but technology designers and developers are working on such kinds of advanced technologies. In fact, Turkle notes that some communities in Japan are moving closer to using robot nannies to care for children and the elderly.[21]

This is part of what McLuhan said about the nature of technology. First we build a technology. Then we begin to imagine expanded possibilities for its uses. Over time, as we implement these possibilities and use the technology, using it starts to change our tastes and preferences. It is comparable to a drink like coffee; many people do not like it at first, but they develop a preference for it over time. Eventually, they value the beverage as if they had always enjoyed it, preferring it to the previous options. This same thing can and does happen with technology. We grow to prefer the technological to the human, and that has the potential to change our interactions with other people and communities. There are benefits and limitations to this dependence on the technology and the context, but it is still important for us to consider these changes and their effects on us and others.

As technologies develop, we continue to devise simulations that mimic the actual world. In fields like education, for example, people are designing digital simulations that allow students to practice real-world skills but without the risk of injury or harm to another person. Simulations for medical students allow them to practice working with patients or performing surgeries without the risk to human life. Flight simulators allow pilots to practice dangerous and complex tactical moves and gain flight experience without the expense and risk of flying an actual aircraft. Many other simulations exist today with thousands more on the way. The role of simulation in education will very likely be a growing part of schools in the near future, just as virtual reality visors are already a part of the gaming world.

Yet, there is another type of simulation that some refer to as "hyperreality," simulations not based upon a real-world thing. They involve simulations that do not directly

21   Ibid., 9–10.

reference reality. As Jean Baudrillard explains and illustrates in his book *Simulacra and Simulation,* hyperreality represents a shift where the fictional comes first, but it takes on the perception of reality. We can go to Disneyland and experience an environment or event in the real world, but everything in that environment or event represents something that is not real. In other circumstances, hyperreality represents something that does not exist, but we act and think as though it does.[22] Those who experience it can find it difficult to distinguish between the hyperreal experience and actual reality. The risk is that people become content substituting the experience of something that is not real in place of the real thing. In fact, one may eventually prefer the hyperreality to actual reality. We value Disneyland more than the real world. We like the way things are in the movies more than what happens in our lives. We appreciate a digitally enhanced version of our physical appearance more than what we see in the mirror. This is not to suggest that it is wrong to enjoy the world of imagination. However, it is important that we are able to distinguish between reality and hyperreality; but that is not always as easy as we might first think.

Consider, for example, the world of celebrity today. Some people become celebrities because of great achievements. Others enjoy a manufactured celebrity. The person is a real and living human being, but his or her public persona is a constructed version. It does not exist in the real world. One example is the way images of models are constructed. Photographers might begin with capturing an image of an actual person. Then the digital editing and touch-ups begin. Experts turn to the computer to remove blemishes, adjust the complexion, lengthen the legs, raise the cheek bones, and narrow the midsection. What we see in a published image of a model might have started with a real person, but at some point, what we look at is the representation of someone who does not and never did exist. This is hyperreality.

Now consider what happens when people do not recognize this fact. We find ourselves idolizing and striving for that which is not real. We create a new standard for beauty. Taken to the extreme, this standard might drive people to take health risks or undergo cosmetic surgery to achieve a desired outcome—and still result in disappointment because the hyperreal never becomes reality. We may obsess about finding or achieving something in our own lives that, in reality, exists only on the screen.

If we look across cultures and throughout history, we will see that humanity has a persistent craving to redesign the human body through piercings, decorative clothing, tattooing, and other such efforts. Today there are countless medical procedures

---

22   Jean Baudrillard, *Simulacra and Simulation,* trans. Sheila Faria Glaser (Ann Arbor: University of Michigan Press, 1994).

available for those who wish to change some aspect of their physical self, to re-create themselves in another image in their mind. Not only are such procedures increasingly common, but they are also becoming more and more acceptable.

This re-creating is not just with the representation of physical appearance. We also see it with the way publicists and agents represent their clients' physical or mental abilities as superhuman. There are indeed many gifted athletes and brilliant minds, but some exaggerate these natural accomplishments to a level that is beyond human reach. Yet, when people do not recognize this difference, they strive to achieve the impossible. They compare themselves to an unrealistic standard.

Among other examples, Baudrillard draws our attention to Disneyland. Designers created it to appear "realistic." But it lacks a connection to the real world. Even though it does not and never did exist in the real world, they have managed to create a physical place where you can experience it as if it were real. You can step into these imaginary worlds for a more immersive experience.

Disneyland is a physical creation intended to represent an imaginary world. In fact, the effort often seems to be creating robotic animals and other experiences that are better than real. Some people prefer them to anything that exists in the real world. They are more vivid and engaging to people than what they encounter outside of the manufactured world. We create a yearning for that which does not actually exist and find ourselves having to settle for boring, dry, flawed, and aging reality. Hyperreality does not aspire to draw us further into real life; instead, it creates an experience that one might come to value more than real life.[23]

This may well seem extreme or far-fetched to some readers. I invite such readers to test this out for themselves. Observe children and others in different contexts, noticing preferences and reactions. Talk to different people about it. I find that young people are often the most candid in discussing their preferences for the hyperreal over the real. What most people will find is a mixed set of preferences. Most children will describe a preference for a real dog to a robotic one, but what if they were at a zoo where there was a sleeping lion or an incredibly realistic robotic one that talked to them, moved constantly, and entertained them in ways that an actual lion would not? This is not to suggest that enjoying the one experience over another is necessarily a problem, but such examples draw our attention to a new phenomenon in our lives, and we can expect such experiences to become increasingly commonplace.

How is this different from enjoying a good movie, an imaginative novel, or a far-fetched play? The distinction is that we approach each of these knowing they are fic-

23   Ibid., 12.

tional. A real-world connection is oftentimes lacking. The consumer, reader, or viewer typically understands that the experience is distinct from the rest of life. Yet, when it comes to hyperreality, the worlds of real and imaginative are blurred.

There is nothing explicitly or morally wrong about the idea of hyperreality, but it still has risks. We may be drawn to build our lives around these unreal worlds, or we might have such strong desires and cravings for something that doesn't exist that we prefer to live as much of our lives as possible in these hyperreal worlds. This might seem like far-fetched science fiction, but we are arriving at a time when the hyperreal is an increasingly common part of life, at least in the context of education and training, and we can expect it to become even more so in the upcoming decades.

The more important action is for us to take time to think and prayerfully consider the benefits and limitations of hyperreality as it becomes a more integrated part of our lives. We do this by engaging in ongoing study of God's Word, seeking His wisdom to help us navigate these changes. We need not jump to conclusions too quickly or establish rules and standards that risk turning into legalism. Yet these changes in our world have implications for how we understand life, what it means to be human, the nature of communication, relationships, and the concept of truth itself.

If we do not take the time to think about and examine these changes, then we risk simply following where the technology leads. We find ourselves becoming comfortable with the changes, so familiar that we cannot objectively analyze the benefits and limitations. We just accept them as a natural part of life, something about which we have little control. These changes might not be explicitly good or bad, but they are also not neutral. They can, do, and will influence our lived experiences, including life in home, church, and community. One way this happens is by subtly shifting our desires toward something hyperreal, like the person who develops a view of beauty based upon the highly edited images of a model instead of what he or she encounters in the real world.

This is no time for anti-intellectualism or a rejection of deep and careful thinking, nor is it a time to forget the limitations of human reason. Yet we can grapple. We can explore. We can discuss. We can seek wisdom from God's Word. In doing so, we discover the persistent relevance of God's Word in modern life, thought, trends, and events. We can make conscious decisions about how we will think and live in these changing times, building our capacity to apply God's Word to circumstances that humankind has never before experienced.

DISCUSSION AND REFLECTION QUESTIONS

- How much do you currently reflect on the affordances and limitations of technology in your life, family, church, workplace, and community?

- To what extent have you seen the emergence of the "robotic moment," when people begin to seek from technology what they previously sought from other people?

- We also examined the concept of hyperreality in this chapter. Do you see examples of this in the world? What concerns do you have about it? What are some promising applications?

WHAT DO YOUR FAVORITE BRANDS SAY ABOUT YOU?

Create a list of your top ten favorite brands. Try to include brands to which you are loyal. You might pick a technology brand like Apple, Google, or Microsoft. It might be your favorite clothing brand, restaurant, grocery store, automobile manufacturer, airline, hotel chain, or shoe brand. What do you admire about these brands? Think about the ideas, beliefs, values, feelings, or emotions you associate with the brand and its products. As you engage in this activity, consider how you associate purchasing or owning products from these brands with what you believe or value in life. This is a helpful exercise in surfacing the role that products and services play in our lives.

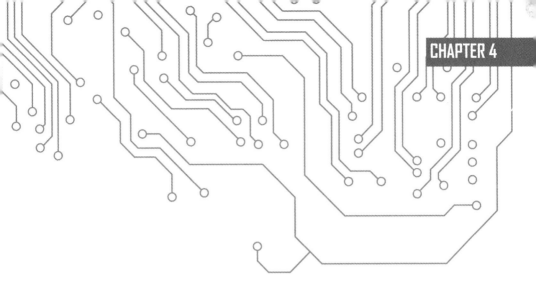

CHAPTER 4

You Are a Consumer and a Product

It is hard to miss the fact that we live in a world of consumerism. We experience a daily encounter with advertisements for vacation destinations, medications, health-care, education, food, cosmetics, and countless other products and services. People are valued for their ability to spend money, to purchase products—to consume—and to produce at ever increasing rates.

Consider the many aspects of American life since the 1920s[24] that more than a few people in the United States take for granted; then look at how the consumerist ideology has influenced those parts of our lives and culture. As a starting point, look at holidays. Valentine's Day is a time to celebrate love and relationships, but the reason it is observed with greeting cards and gifts is because doing so is good for business. The same can be said for some Christian holidays. Christmas has a widespread, even central, focus on the purchase of gifts. Easter, on buying special candy. Beyond these are the many secular holidays that are gift-giving occasions: Boss's Day, Administrative Professionals' Day, Grandparents Day—and the big ones—Mother's Day and Father's Day. Each of these, while ostensibly occasions to recognize and appreciate the people in our lives, originate in the drive to get more people to buy more things.

In the aftermath of grief, fear, and loss following the 9/11 terrorist attacks on the United States, we faced economic uncertainty. To prevent an economic downturn, President George W. Bush challenged Americans to go out and shop (among other

---

24   I selected the Roaring Twenties because that decade is often described as the era in which American consumerism began; however, there is certainly an argument to be made that con-sumerism was re-created by the emergence of the Internet in the 1990s, the decade in which some massive online retail sources like Amazon emerged.

things).[25] It is not every day that Americans have the bonus justification of shopping as a civic or patriotic duty. President Bush's suggestion was neither right nor wrong, but it does reflect how our society depends heavily upon consumerism to keep things running smoothly.

At its worst, a worldview we often encounter or hold dear says, "The winners in life are those who accumulate the most possessions." Owning and consuming have become sources of identity and worth for us. Possessions are not just physical objects; they say something about who we are, who we want to be, what we value, where we find meaning, and more. While most of us balk at those statements, a scan of our lives suggests that many of us live as if this is true. Buying and owning extends far beyond necessity.

We build our identities and others' identities around possessions. The car we drive, the clothes we wear, the size and location of our house says something about us and about other people from our perception. The latest and greatest devices we stand in line to purchase and the designer handbags we carry say something about us. These things represent the image we convey to ourselves and to those around us. The content (print and digital) we subscribe to is not just about information that interests us. They also reflect an image that resonates with us. All of these aspects of our lives remind us that consumerism is embedded in our views of life, work, family, and community. We are not just consumers because we buy items from others instead of making them for ourselves. We are consumers because the accumulation of an increasing number of goods and services is a significant part of American culture. For many, shopping is a hobby, not just a necessity.

But we are not just consumers in this modern landscape. We ourselves are also products. Consider the business model of Google. While many think of Google as a search engine, it is primarily an advertising company. Organizations and individuals pay Google to place ads in front of people whose search histories most closely align with what the advertisers have to sell. Most of us realize that when we use Google to look for something, our search histories and any demographic data in our social media profiles are collected for advertising purposes. The first items that show up on our searches are usually paid ads from companies. Companies may pay fifty dollars or more to get us to click on their ads so they can try to convince us to buy their products.

Our attention is for sale, and that is no small part of the online experience. Yes, there is an incomprehensible amount of free content available online, but the platform on which that free content is shared needs a viable financial model. YouTube, for ex-

---

25 "President Bush's News Conference," *New York Times*, December 20, 2006, http://www.nytimes.com/2006/12/20/washington/20text-bush.html (accessed March 19, 2017).

ample, did not initially focus on creating content. It was originally a forum on which people could store and share their video content with others. Over time, though, YouTube's developers saw the opportunity for revenue by creating pop-up and embedded advertisements with the video content.

Jason Fitzpatrick explained this well in the title of his Lifehacker article: "If You're Not Paying for It, You're the Product."[26] The Internet is not all business, but business drives much of what we think of as the Internet. This is true from our email accounts to our use of Google products to Facebook, Twitter, Pinterest, and many other social media sites. All of these represent financial interests, and although you are not explicitly paying for a service, that service is most often not free. You are, in one way or another, the product. Businesses capture and monetize your search habits. Companies sell your attention to other companies that want to sell something to you.

An ever-increasing amount of profiling based on our online activities is taking place. For example, some sources claim that Facebook analytics are so accurate that they can predict a person's sexual orientation, political leanings, and shopping preferences simply based on the sites visited, searches conducted, friends followed, and products and resources that capture his or her attention online.[27]

There are, of course, individuals and organizations that are not in it for the money. And there are those that need revenue to keep functioning but do not have the purpose of making a profit. Wikipedia, for example, is a not-for-profit organization that depends upon volunteers, donations, and grants to keep running. It also generates needed income by selling advertising space.[28] On a much smaller scale, there are bloggers, writing about countless topics, who have no interest in monetizing their work. They just want to have a voice or share an area of passion or expertise with the world. There are also many online communities in which people gather around a shared interest simply to connect, not to make money from the interaction. They value the community, the learning, the entertainment, and the connections with others that the Internet provides.

Even in these cases, however, we are wise to remember that much of the digital age is dependent upon moneymaking. Although people may not be earning money from a blog or an online community, someone or some business in the infrastructure of that

---

26   Jason Fitzpatrick, "If You're Not Paying for It, You're the Product," *Lifehacker*, November 23, 2010, http://lifehacker.com/5697167/if-youre-not-paying-for-it-youre-the-product (accessed March 19, 2017).

27   Geoffrey Mohan, "On Facebook, You Are What You 'Like,' Study Finds," *Los Angeles Times*, March 11, 2013, http://articles.latimes.com/2013/mar/11/science/la-sci-facebook-likes-20130312 (accessed March 19, 2017).

28   "Frequently asked questions," *Wikimedia Foundation*, https://wikimediafoundation.org/wiki/FAQ/en#Where_does_my_money_go.3F (accessed March 19, 2017).

online product or service is generating revenue. Again, if you are online, you are either a consumer or a product or often both.

I do not write any of this to argue for or against a capitalist society or a digital age, but to challenge readers to be alert to the models that drive this digital age. This is part of living the examined life in a digital and connected era. We can use this knowledge to make decisions that best align with our goals, beliefs, and convictions. While our culture of consumerism might naturally drive us to enjoy a life of shopping and consuming, there are times when such a lifestyle might interfere with our desire to tithe or financially support a ministry or charity that is important us. We might be driven to work overtime and longer hours to support a lifestyle of consumerism, but discover that this extra work also draws us away from precious time that we value with family, friends, and our church communities. We might find it difficult to invest in the cost of a Christian education because of our desire to spend that money on other products and services. As I mentioned earlier in the book, it is very easy for what I just wrote to come off as legalistic, piling a new moral standard beyond what Scripture commands or forbids. That is not my intent. I simply offer these examples to illustrate ways in which our careful and prayerful consideration can help us to align lifestyle decisions with our beliefs and values.

At the same time, it would indeed be a travesty if we submitted to the idea that we define our identity and value by this consumer-driven web. It might be true that many companies value us as products online, but that is not the source of our ultimate worth. We are so much more than a product and a consumer. As Christians, we know that our core identity is in Jesus Christ. "For God so loved the world, that He gave His only Son, that whoever believes in Him should not perish but have eternal life" (John 3:16). This Bible verse, so well-known to many of us, speaks to our worth in God's eyes. To use a financial metaphor, God was willing to pay a price for each of us that is far greater than the cost of any advertisement on the web. While the companies behind advertising are engaging in pricing battles for our attention, God paid for us with the precious blood of His only-begotten Son.

This may be a startling message to some readers and a simple and incredibly familiar message to others. It is, nonetheless, an important one for us to keep in mind. Whatever words, graphics, or slogans companies create and present to us to garner our attention or our money, we have a God whose attention is always ours, with genuine authenticity—no hidden agendas at work—always seeking and providing for our best interest. This grounds us in the important truth that our identity is hidden in Christ—

who gave us what we really need, which is also the most fulfilling and permanent good we could ever have—not in the goods and services we consume.

DISCUSSION AND REFLECTION QUESTIONS

- In what ways, if any, do you struggle with defining your worth or identity on the basis of what you own and accumulate?

- Can you think of examples of the consumer-driven identity finding its way into your home, church, school, and community?

- Prior to reading this chapter, how aware were you of the consumer-driven nature of our online lives? How does this alter or confirm the way you think about online activities?

DO YOU EXIST ONLINE?

The Laodicean effect depends upon people, churches, and organizations being willing to create and share content online. People can discover only what exists. As far as the digital world is concerned, if you are not a creator of content, a curator of content, or a contributor to online communities, then you do not exist in that world. That means that your beliefs, values, and viewpoints are not discoverable for others. Yet, this is an age when people are literally turning to Google for answers about some of their most pressing questions in life, even questions about the existence of God, why bad things happen to seemingly good people, and where to go for guidance on moral decisions. Can people find you online? Do you have something to say that might be a blessing or benefit to others? Where and how might you share that?

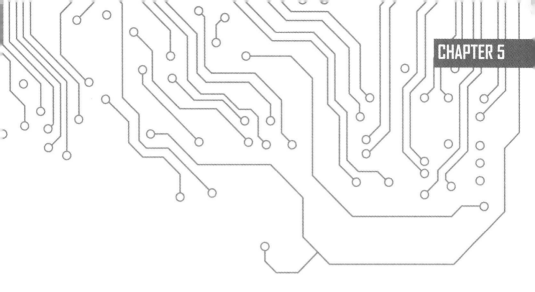

CHAPTER 5

The Laodicean Effect

I used to study the myriad search terms related to religion and spirituality. I used various tools provided by Google and other search engines that allowed me to see which terms were trending on a particular day. This helped me get a better sense of what religious themes were popular in the digital world; it also allowed me to see how people were using the web as part of their religious explorations.

It did not take long to learn that people do indeed Google "God." Just as we turn to YouTube or Google for information about all sorts of things, our efforts at learning about spiritual matters are no different. Every minute of every day, people go to a search engine with their most pressing questions: "Does God exist?" "Why does God allow bad things to happen to good people?" "What is the meaning of life?" "Are angels real?"

In the summer of 2009, as I was looking at the fastest growing keyword trends in religion over the preceding thirty days, I was surprised to see the word "Laodicean" was at the top of the list. If you are not familiar with it, Laodicea shows up in Colossians 2:1 and 4:13–16 and also near the beginning of the Book of Revelation. The Church of Laodicea was the one to receive that firm correction, "Because you are lukewarm, and neither hot nor cold, I will spit you out of my mouth" (Revelation 3:16). I was puzzled. This is a rather obscure word to be trending (meaning thousands of people or more were researching it). What could possibly explain such a thing?

I wondered, "Is there still a Laodicea today that is in the news? Hopefully there wasn't some sort of terrorist attack or natural disaster." The town referred to in Revelation does not exist today. I typed "Laodicea" into Google, but that took me in the wrong direction. Then I typed the exact word that was trending: "Laodicean." Lo and behold, what came up was an image of a thirteen-year-old girl, Kavya Shivashankar of Olathe, Kansas, standing on a stage.[29]

Why that specific image? My search took me to a May 29, 2009, article titled "'Laodicean' launches Kansas teen to spelling bee victory."[30] There you have it. A bright young person wins the National Spelling Bee on the word *Laodicean*, and the web lights up with people around the United States searching a word that otherwise rarely is mentioned. You can picture it. People are watching the final round of the National Spelling Bee on television, and this word comes up. The contestant spells it correctly and is crowned the champ, but the viewers are curious. What does this word mean? So, they head to the Internet.

When they did that search, what do you think they found? There are not many websites dedicated to Laodicea, fewer even in 2009. Yet, there are websites that mention Laodicea: namely, those created by pastors and Bible study leaders talking about the Book of Revelation. Can you picture it? Suddenly, rarely visited websites about the Church in Laodicea are getting thousands of visitors. Who knows how many people ended up on random websites and read about God's dissatisfaction when people who have heard His Word are neither hot nor cold, are spiritually complacent?

Consider this possibility: A woman living in Los Angeles, who went to church as a child but stopped attending a long time ago, was enjoying a little television. Switching through the channels, she came across the National Spelling Bee and decided to watch it. As she did, she heard the word *Laodicean* spelled correctly by the spelling bee winner. Out of curiosity, she pulled out her phone and searched the word on Google. The first link to appear was to a Bible study placed online by a pastor in a small church in rural Alaska with a typical Sunday attendance of twenty-five people. She clicked on the link and read about the Laodiceans and the related Bible passage in the Book of Revelation. As she read, she found herself wanting to read more. So, she found an online Bible, since she no longer owned a hard copy, and began to read it. The more she read, the more she wanted to read. For the next week, what she had read kept coming to mind, occupying her thoughts and raising questions.

A couple of weeks later, on a Sunday morning, she decided to go to a nearby church. It was awkward and even a bit scary for her, but she went. While there, she met a person

29   Associated Press, "Kansas girl Kavya Shivashankar wins Scripps National Spelling Bee by getting 'Laodicean' right," NY Daily News, May 28, 2009, http://www.nydailynews.com/news/world/kansas-girl-kavya-shivashankar-wins-scripps-national-spelling-bee-laodicean-article-1.412870 (accessed March 19, 2017).

30   "'Laodicean' launches Kansas teen to spelling bee victory," CNN.com, May 29, 2009, http://www.cnn.com/2009/US/05/28/national.spelling.bee/ (accessed March 19, 2017).

her age who lived a few blocks away, and they went out for coffee. As they shared their stories, they realized they enjoyed each other's company. The two became friends and met for coffee after church for the next several weeks. Fast forward six months, and this woman regularly attends church, has made several new friends, and is developing a deep and vibrant faith in Jesus. To think that something like this can start with an unfamiliar word from a spelling bee. Imagine the possibilities in the world of faith and life in a digital age!

This might be some strange social media equivalent of the butterfly effect, which proposes that a butterfly flapping its wings on one side of the planet can cause a chain reaction of events, even a tsunami on the other side of the planet.[31] When something like this occurs in the digital world, I propose that we rename it "the Laodicean effect." For example, could a girl from Kansas who spells a word correctly on a stage in Washington, DC, really cause such a flurry of Internet activity that a woman in Los Angeles makes the connection between a town that existed two thousand years ago in Turkey to something that exists today, a Las Vegas–style, action-packed social hot spot? Could this event lead to a significant spiritual transformation for that woman living in California, a stranger living hundreds of miles away from the teenage girl from Kansas? While this is a fictional thought experiment, the answer appears to be yes. And how about the irony of an ancient community known for being neither hot nor cold turning into the hottest (i.e., fastest-growing) religious topic on the web for a month in 2009?

The Laodicean effect represents two forms of connection among people in the digital age. Of course, connecting across increasingly greater distances is not new among humanity, nor is it new for the Church. Consider the way in which the Christian faith passed from one person to another in the first century. Paul and others became the first Christian missionaries by traveling among the Roman world and verbally sharing the Gospel, but passing letters from one location to another played a rather large role in the spread of the Gospel as well. Then, in the sixteenth century, the printing press was critical in the production and, therefore, distribution of books and pamphlets about the Christian faith. Five hundred years later, we have radio, telephone, television. And now mobile devices, smart devices in our homes, and countless communication technologies associated with the Internet make it possible to have real-time or nearly real-time communication across thousands of miles.

These communication technologies give anyone with Internet access a voice and platform unlike any other time in history. A teenage girl can create YouTube videos

---

31 Edward N. Lorenz, *The Essence of Chaos* (Seattle: University of Washington Press, 2008), 179–82.

about makeup, Minecraft, or anything else, and it can be viewed by hundreds of thousands of people. Anyone with a little know-how can create a website or a blog or develop a strong public presence on a dozen or more social media sites, giving them the potential to influence others in ways we cannot imagine.

Notice that there are at least two different types of influence prevalent throughout social media: the corporate or well-resourced organizations that use these communication tools to influence their constituents, and the democratized media technologies (as I call them), the means by which anyone with Internet access or data plan on their phone can communicate messages that people all over the world read, hear, or watch. Let us look at each of these dynamics a little more closely.

THE INFLUENCE OF THE POWERFUL AND WELL-RESOURCED

Consider the way that elections take place today. Candidates spend millions of dollars to create advertisements across all media outlets. They debate on national television. The hire public relations experts to pitch stories to the mainstream news in the hope of getting more publicity. They create a robust online presence via their use of various social media platforms. Again, they spend *millions* to create a campaign across various media, and they do it because it works. It influences people.

Alternatively, consider that large companies have multimillion-dollar budgets to promote their products and services. They buy space for print ads and air time for television commercials. They pay for product placements in films and television shows. They pay for online advertisements that track with key words and follow you around the web. They create a robust marketing strategy across these and other outlets to increase awareness of and interest in what they have to sell.

This strategy goes beyond political campaigns and companies trying to sell things. Some organizations use the same approach to shape public opinion on social, moral, and religious issues. This can be done by simply paying for increased exposure of their preferred position to make it seem mainstream. It can be done by spinning comments to put people who disagree with the position in a negative light. For example, some people represent Christians as judgmental, closed-minded, and anti-intellectual. They do not need to state this explicitly (although some spokespeople get pretty close). They only need to shape the way people receive the message through creative, subtle efforts.

THE EVERYDAY PERSON

While having millions of dollars certainly allows politicians and corporations to influence and communicate unlike any other time in history, even more novel is the fact that any individual can have significant influence with only the cost of a device and an Internet connection. A middle-aged man who lives in a small city and works at the local bike repair shop by day but has a YouTube channel can have a following of tens of thousands of people by singing songs from his living room, giving bike repair tips, or just inviting people to watch him play video games while he comments on what is happening.

If you look at the blogosphere (the vast world of blogs and their interconnectedness), you may notice a genre known as "Mommy Blogs." These blogs are created by moms who write about all sorts of topics: balancing work and family, cooking, hobbies, parenting, travel, politics, financial tips, or celebrities and entertainment. Some bloggers have turned what may have begun as a hobby into a six-figure business, making money by selling products, allowing advertisements on their site, having corporate sponsors for their work, or generating speaking and consulting opportunities. The "Mommy Blog" group is a powerful social force in the digital age, collectively gleaning millions of daily visitors. Even one mommy blogger who sets aside three to five hours a week may have thousands of daily visitors to her blog. We find similar expressions in all sorts of video sharing, image sharing, micro-blogging, and other social media outlets, some of which might have come into existence since the time of this book's publication. The reality of the capacity to influence through social media is not news to many of us, but that makes it even more important for us to pause and consider the benefits, limitations, and implications.

Any individual has the ability to share messages that are read from almost anywhere in the world. When people establish an online presence, they have no idea whom they might influence and how they might influence them. This truly is the Laodicean effect, and I have experienced it personally.

More than a decade ago, I started a blog called Etale.org to share what I was thinking and discovering about life and learning in the digital age. For the first few years, I did not take it very seriously. I posted something every week or two. Sometimes I went months without posting. Yet, in the last five years, I decided to devote more time to it, writing and sharing two to four articles every week. Within a year, I had almost 100,000 unique visitors attending my blog and reading my articles. I started to get emails from people all over the world. This led to speaking invitations, consulting jobs, requests for help from students, and so many other connections. This all comes from spending a few hours a week writing about what I am thinking and learning, and publishing my thoughts online.

This is possible for anyone in the digital age regardless of age, gender, educational background, location, ethnicity, or ability. People use digital opportunities to share positive or negative messages, to connect with like-minded people, to create new opportunities for themselves, and also to communicate their messages in the hope of spreading their beliefs and values, whatever those may be.

We cannot always anticipate the influence or impact of such digital efforts. Yet, we can be certain of two things: the digital world is a part of people's lives, and it has an impact upon their beliefs and values. When people turn to the web with even their most personal questions and concerns, what will they find? This is an important question for us to consider as we think about our role as Christians in the digital world. When Jesus said, "Go into all nations," does that include the digital world as well? We will explore these questions of how Christians can best relate to the digital world in the second part of this book.

DISCUSSION AND REFLECTION QUESTIONS

- In what ways do you see digital culture influencing your daily life?
- How do you see digital culture influencing your family?
- Do you see digital culture shaping or influencing your church?
- How do you see technology influencing the beliefs and values of people in your community or workplace?

WHAT DOES YOUR NEWS SAY ABOUT YOU?

As we will explore in this next chapter, there are seemingly endless sources of news today. What are your go-to sources? Consider the many ways in which you consume news—from traditional evening news on television to websites, blogs, Facebook, Twitter, YouTube, content aggregators like Feedly or the Apple News app, podcasts, Pinterest, Instagram, LinkedIn, or maybe traditional newspapers or magazines. Make a list of your preferred sources. Why do you prefer these over others? What are the benefits and limitations to your news sources?

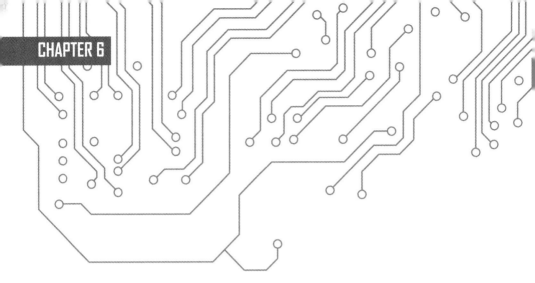

CHAPTER 6

The Daily Me

There used to be the idea of the daily news. People woke up in the morning, re-trieved their local newspaper from the front yard, and read it over breakfast or a cup of coffee. From there they headed to work. What they read in the paper served as shared information about current events in that city and around the world. If they did not read the newspaper, they listened to the radio or watched one of a half-dozen television shows to get the news. What one person read, watched, or heard via one news source paralleled what others read, watched, or heard. Millions of people went through the day with a shared vocabulary and understanding of significant events in their communities and around the world. Daily news was a shared point of reference for much of society.

Dissemination of news still exists today, obviously. When something significant happens, the news media report it. There is enough news in common that we still have a sense of shared significant events. What has changed is that today we have an expansive array of news outlets and perspectives from which people can choose.

Of course, there has always been a limitation to this concept of the daily news. When there were only a few news sources dominating the attention of public, we had access to only a few perspectives of a given story. We all heard the same news report. If those in charge of the news determined something was not newsworthy or did not serve the public's best interest, then the public remained unaware. The news media has wielded great power and responsibility and still does. They can draw attention to one topic and away from another. They shape public opinion by what they report and how they report it. Even when they are trying to be neutral, the simple decision to report on one story and not another is far from unbiased.

People who create the news can change mindsets and agendas and influence people's emotional state. In *How to Watch the TV News,* Neil Postman and Steve Powers explain this fact with the following example: The early twentieth-century journalist Lincoln Steffens proved he could create a "crime wave" anytime he wanted, simply by writing about all the crimes that normally occur in a large city during the course of a month. He could also end the crime wave by not writing about them.[32] That is, when we hear story after story about crime, we are more likely to think about crime and assume it is prevalent, even if we do not witness or experience any actual crime. When we do not hear such stories and do not experience actual crime, we tend to see the community as safer. This seems like common sense, but we often do not realize how much the news influences what occupies our thoughts—which in turn influences our actions—and, therefore, how much responsibility to communicate truth the news carries.

What happens when news sources represent matters of morality and religion? Can we attribute the growing expanse of beliefs and values to strategic and intentional efforts to expose these beliefs and values in more favorable and comfortable formats through talk shows, news stories, documentaries, and other forms of media? The question, of course, is whether we will allow our beliefs and values to be shaped by the dominant narratives in the media or whether we will, like the Bereans, test what we hear against the Scriptures.

In this digital age, the means by which we get our news are more varied than ever due to the incredible diversity of sources we are able to access online. One person reads a daily newspaper, listens to a favorite conservative news show on the radio, and scans the stories at CNN.com. Another subscribes to a grassroots news outlet that sends breaking stories to his email inbox. The next person frequents a collection of conspiracy theory podcasts and websites. Still another gets the majority of news from social media updates. Then there is one more person who watches news clips of a favorite talk show that connects comedy and current events, perhaps supplemented from a weekly scan of stories at the BBC and Al Jazeera websites. There will be some things in common among these news sources, but these people are less likely to experience shared stories and shared perspectives than in the past. This might not reflect your news source choices, but that is part of my point. Every person today has an incredibly wide range of sources from which to choose, and people do just that—they choose diverse sources. Most might not think of a person who scans news sources from a mix of comedy news, the BBC, and also Al Jazeera, but there is no question that various people do indeed blend together such diverse sources today.

32   Neil Postman and Steve Powers, *How to Watch TV News* (New York: Penguin Books, 2008), 24.

There are benefits and limitations to this, of course. In the past, a relatively small number of powerful media outlets controlled the daily, collective narratives and had greater influence on the public's attention and worldview than most other entities. Today, while many media outlets continue to approach news with integrity and responsibility, others will be driven by what makes good news, increases ratings and viewership, or benefits the core mission and goals of the outlet and its owners.

The number of media outlets continues to expand, giving even greater voice and influence not only to corporations but also to individuals. I can attest to this personally. As I mentioned earlier, more than a decade ago I launched a blog where I published my informal thoughts, reflections, and ideas related to life and learning in an increasingly digital context. For the first five years, I wrote infrequently and few people visited the blog. But as I wrote more consistently, often sharing links to my articles on other social media outlets, traffic to my blog increased. To date, more than a million people have visited my blog. That is not some major news outlet; it is one person with a laptop and Internet access.

All of this came from less than a $100 investment in the technologies and resources needed to get started. I had no investors. I do not own a large media company. Of course, I also do not have a readership or viewership of millions. Yet I am able to share news and insights with a rather large group of people around the world, with more than a thousand people subscribing to receive updates when I add anything to my blog.

Now consider the millions of new blog posts published each day by all the bloggers out there, numbering between one and two hundred million.[33] Add to that the people who post YouTube videos, Tweet, post Facebook updates, and contribute to other social media outlets such as Instagram and Snapchat. Then consider the number of small and grassroots news and information outlets and resources that exist, representing just about every political, religious, and ideological perspective imaginable. That is the current landscape of news media.

This leads us back to the idea of "the daily me."[34] Each of us selects from a vast smorgasbord of news sources. Some are more reliable than others. The amount of bias varies. Some align with our beliefs and values, while others do not. Some report the news in an abbreviated, straightforward manner, while others infuse ample explanation

---

33 "Blogging Statistics," Worldometers, March 15, 2017, http://www.worldometers.info/blogs (accessed March 19, 2017).

34 The term comes from a project described in the following article, though the phrase "the daily me" is being used here in a different way from its original content. Christopher Harper, "The Daily Me," *American Journalism Review*, April 1997, http://ajrarchive.org/Article.asp?id=268 (accessed March 19, 2017).

or commentary from a distinct perspective. We draw from our favorite sources, creating a personalized news feed. There may be crossover among some news reports, but we no longer have only a handful of shared news stories from common perspectives—and that has both benefits and limitations. How do we make sense of this?

I experienced this daily me back in 2010 when I was speaking to a group of school leaders about the impact of technology on the beliefs and values of young people. During my keynote, I shared a story about an experience I had years before during a trip to Haiti. While there, I visited an orphanage of young children, some of whom had serious health concerns. I explained how I lifted up a boy who was four or five years old, but I felt like I was picking up an infant. He was skin and bones, and he hardly reacted to anything I did. Yet, when I had to leave and went to put him down, he came to life, screaming and reaching out to me to hold him again. It was an incredibly emotional moment for me, and I shared this story to this group of school teachers to illustrate a point.

I had talked about my Haiti trip in the past, but this time was different. I saw people in the audience tearing up as I told the story. After my keynote ended, a number of people came up to talk about the story I'd just told. The first person who came up to me said something like "Thank you for speaking today. The story you shared about Haiti was powerful, especially given the news headlines yesterday." What news? I had been out of touch with the most recent world news. After the event, on the way to the airport, I had to check out this news. I searched Haiti online and a list of stories about a terribly destructive earthquake with rising death tolls filled my screen. I had no idea any of this was happening.

How is that possible? At that point, in 2010, Google offered a feature called iGoogle. It was a sort of personalized homepage. You could set it to feed favorite news sources and topics, new posts from favorite blogs, local weather, and several other options. It all showed up on what was like a personalized front page of a digital newspaper, updated by the minute. I did not include any major news sources on my page at the time. I instead focused upon information from blogs, research journals, and other things directly related to my research. I was laser focused on those matters. That was helpful to my work, but it also resulted in self-exclusion from many significant national and global events. I was, therefore, largely uninformed about important matters in my local community, country, and world. This is an example of how we can use news and knowledge sources as a lens for seeing the world.

"The daily me" is real. "The daily me" consists of a personally curated set of news and sources instead of turning to a prepackaged news source. It certainly represents a change in collective culture in that we no longer experience shared information and narratives with the people around us. Instead we control the information, filter it by our interests and worldview, and shut out anything we don't want to see.

This culture is exacerbated by fake news, alternative facts, and increasingly biased news and information sources. In today's news environment, I am just as likely to learn about what is happening in the world from a friend, colleague, family member, or someone in my extended network online as I am from an informed journalist through a traditional media outlet. Sometimes information comes in the form of a Tweet with a 140-character commentary and a link to an article on another online news source. Even that Tweet changes the way I encounter and think about the topic because it is biased. The reliability of news sources highlights the importance of media literacy, information literacy, and critical thinking as important parts of our formative education.

I had a proud moment when my daughter (who was six or seven years old at the time) and I were watching a television show together. A commercial came on that promoted a popular doll. It was bright pink, cheerful, and certainly captured my daughter's interest. Conflicted, she looked to me and said, "Daddy, I know they are trying to trick me to buy it, but sometimes it is okay to be tricked, right?"

"Sometimes it is okay to be tricked." Now that is a statement worth unpacking. Of course, what she meant is that the commercial was persuasive, she wanted the doll, and while she understood the intent and even a few of the strategies employed in the commercial, it still worked on her. The good news to me was that she was becoming self-aware; she understood that even watching something as seemingly harmless as a doll commercial calls for cultivating a type of literacy.

Literacy means more than vocabulary and decoding the meaning of words and sentences. Literacy today involves participating in conversations across various media. Like learning a language, it includes cultural components, countless nuances, beliefs, values, and logic. We live in a world in which some news sources intentionally present stories and ideas in ways that are less connected to reality. Some are playful and satirical commentaries. Others are strategic tactics to influence and misinform. Some are both.

When I was working on my doctorate, I took an instructional design class where I opted to create an online tutorial to teach students about information and media literacy. I created a series of fake news pages and set up a game requiring students to analyze the pages using a checklist I provided. Students were instructed to rate each source and argue whether it was reliable and useful for various purposes. To make it interesting,

I included links to real news sources I did not create. At the time, many larger online news sources used formulaic site designs, so it was easy to replicate the look and feel of legitimate sites when designing my fake sites.

It was an enlightening exercise for all of us. I was surprised at the difficulty many students had identifying the fake sites. Students, of course, were developing a view of what it means to consume information on the web. For me, this exercise began what turned into more than fifteen years of studying media and information literacy.

The term *fake news* is a recent addition to our lexicon, but it refers to spoofs and hoaxes that have been a part of the publishing and news industries for centuries. In the twenty-first century though, the term means the intentional misinformation that gives the perception and has the intention of substituting for reputable news. Fake news might be generated by a lack of research, the fault of the writer to check his or her biased approach to a topic, or to intentional deception to achieve a desired end. It gets complicated when so many people point to others as sources of fake news.

Learning to identify a fake news story or unreliable source is more important than ever, especially with social media as a prominent means by which people discover news. Yet, identifying it is not necessarily—or easily—done with a checklist. Discernment calls for learning about logical fallacies and reading across different media. It requires becoming fluent enough in these areas to see nuances, just as we do when we are fluent in a language. A few media literacy tutorials are not enough; it happens only with persistent, authentic, immersive, and ongoing exploration.

Alternative Facts

The concept of alternative facts arose in 2017 around claims that major news outlets were not telling the truth. In one famous moment, a representative of President Donald Trump said that, while the news media claims to have facts, the Trump administration has "alternative facts."[35] Detractors jumped on this comment right away, claiming that it is the mind-set of a totalitarian regime, but it can be said that such a characterization is, in itself, a form of misinformation.

While I reference the events of the 2017 election because that is where this concept of "alternative facts" gained widespread attention, it is not something new, nor is it tied to a specific political party or position. Rather, it is reflective of our current situation where there are more contrasting and conflicting news sources available to us than at

35   Aaron Blake, "Kellyanne Conway Says Donald Trump's Team Has 'Alternative Facts.' Which Pretty Much Says It All," *The Washington Post*, January 22, 2017, https://www.washingtonpost.com/news/the-fix/wp/2017/01/22/kellyanne-conway-says-donald-trumps-team-has-alternate-facts-which-pretty-much-says-it-all/?utm_term=.ff653fd2db4d (accessed March 19, 2017).

any other time in history. Pick any major world event, and we can find news reports that describe the event in ways that are so different that we find ourselves wondering what actually occurred. On the global scale, we can see that by how textbooks and popular information sources in different parts of the world retell events such as World War II, for instance. The way young people learn about World War II in the United States is most certainly distinct from how it is represented in the United Kingdom, France, Germany, Japan, and Russia.

The Dangers of Personal News Aggregation

Another aspect of news today resulting from the lack of go-to news sources is the effect of disconnected stories and narratives. More than ever, we are gathering our news and information from many different sources and contexts. This is where we originally got the idea of "surfing" the web. This means we are jumping contexts. It is as though one room in your house is New York City, but when you walk into the next room, you are in the streets of Tehran. Go down the stairs and you are in rural Wisconsin. Keep going to the kitchen, and now you are in Washington, DC. Each of those contexts is different enough that it is not possible to treat them all the same, and we run into this when we consume news and information online—it is disparate and disjointed. This, I contend, calls for an entirely new set of skills, literacies, and ways of thinking. Developing these skills empowers us as individuals to curate our own news sources, but it also risks intentionally siloing ourselves from different viewpoints.

The Dangers of Algorithmic News Aggregation

Much of the web today runs on algorithms that automatically choose content for us based on our viewing history, profiles, preferences, and other demographic data collected about us. This is how each person's exploration of the web is personalized. Some of what we see is driven by paid advertisements. This hidden system also determines which news sites are a good fit for us based on our search history and social media activity. Those who create and control the algorithm might even use it in an effort to influence us. It can draw our attention to some things and away from others. It might have the appearance of personal news aggregation when the system is actually doing much of the selection. I do not want to make this sound more sinister than it is, but we should not ignore the potential for abuse, misuse, and manipulation by those who are able to control which news sites and stories do or do not appear on Facebook and other social media outlets that feed us stories and content.

From the outset of civilization, commentary and editorials have been part of news and knowledge sources, but today it is off the charts. Most major news sources have platforms dedicated to editorials and commentaries on news events. There is a steady stream of commentary in written, visual, and multimedia formats across current and emerging social media outlets. On top of that are news sources that mix entertainment and news. Many of us first learn about news by finding it embedded in these commentaries. Do we go to the original sources to make sense of it ourselves? Do we come to rely on our favorite or trusted commentators to interpret the news for us? This is a major part of discourse in a connected age, and digital citizenship calls for us to make sense of it, to analyze it, and to discern truth.

The fact that the Internet is now the first place many of us go when we have a question or want to learn something new further highlights the importance of discernment. Take these common scenarios: You and a family member are arguing about some fact or idea at the dinner table. When you cannot come to a resolution, what happens? More often than not, one of you will pull out your phone or go over to the computer to resolve the dispute with some facts. A student who is struggling with an answer to a problem or question turns to a search engine to find the answer. Many turn to Google, Wikipedia, or YouTube. We are rarely far from a means of searching for information via the Internet.

This same activity is increasingly true for spiritual questions and matters of religion. While some still turn to a pastor or trusted and knowledgeable family member, the readily accessible Internet is changing our spiritual development as well. When someone goes to a favorite search engine and types in a question, what will show up? What answers will he or she find? Will these answers lead him or her to or away from the truth revealed in the Scriptures?

There is little evidence that this is slowing or changing. In fact, new technologies allow us to skip the effort of typing a question into a search engine and just speak it aloud. If you have an Apple device, you just ask Siri and she draws from her database to give you an answer or offer websites that can help. If you have a Windows device, it might be Cortana that answers your request. If you have an Android device or smart speaker that gives you instant access by voice command, you can ask Google Now. Then there is Amazon's Alexa. Of course, this technology is changing so quickly that there may well be many other options by the time you are reading this book.

It is not always clear who provides the answers, and the biases included in those answers are not always apparent. Sometimes answers are benign and factual, but at other times, there is room for interpretation. Even when the information is factual, there is always the question of what is included and what is omitted. That alone can influence what and how we think. So, what happens when people turn to these digital assistants and search engines as their first source when they wonder about the existence of God, the nature of good versus evil, moral questions, and countless other spiritual matters?

These are important questions for us to ponder as Christians, as family members, and as a congregation—and they bring us back to Christian discernment. The rapid-fire way information comes at us can overwhelm our ability to analyze and understand it. Some of us develop a near addiction to seeking out more information, binging upon source after source. Amid this barrage of information, do we take the time to consider what is true? to ponder how it compares or contrasts with the unchanging truths of God's Word? How do we cultivate an ability to assess trustworthiness of news sources, the accuracy of claims, and ultimately how it will inform how we live out our vocations? We will return to this and many other issues in the second part of the book as we consider how to respond to such trends.

DISCUSSION AND REFLECTION QUESTIONS

- How do you stay informed in this digital age? How is that similar to or different from methods in the past?

- How has the growth of "alternative facts" and "fake news" affected the way you consume and assess news?

- Describe an example or two of how "fake news" has influenced you or those around you.

- How do you go about evaluating the bias and reliability of news you consume?

HAVE YOU USED THE POWER OF ONLINE CONNECTIONS AS A TOOL FOR GOOD?

Think about the different reasons you connect or collaborate with people online. Perhaps it is a pastime, part of your work, or something else. Think back over your online activities over the last few months or even the last year. Can you identify ways in which you or others you know have used the power of online connections or collaborations to show love for others, to help with a worthy cause, or to share the love of God in Christ? How did you do it? What worked well and what did not? What opportunities do you have to use online connections for good today, this week, or this month?

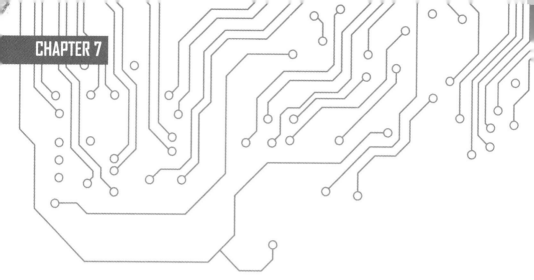

CHAPTER 7

Smart Mobs and Pools of Ignorance

The development of an increasingly digital and technological world creates far more ways for people connect and collaborate. There are online communities specific to teachers, lawyers, healthcare professionals, computer programmers, artists, and taxidermists. There are networks and communities for people who have migraines, who are cancer survivors, who are living with diabetes, and who struggle with depression, and the list goes on. There are communities and networks for people who love to bake, remodel old homes, knit, love cats, live off the grid (yes, there is some irony in this one), make jewelry, play a particular video game, collect stamps (or anything else), and love Harry Potter. Speaking of Harry Potter, there are fan-fiction communities for thousands of films, books, and television shows. Some of these communities existed prior to the Internet, but participation was largely limited by time and place. Now, on any given day, we can connect with others who share similar experiences or interests.

If a community related to your need or interest does not already exist, there are dozens of ways you can create one in minutes. Or you can wait; new networks and communities emerge every day for recreational purposes, for personal development, and to accomplish professional tasks. Typically, these networks are voluntary and democratic in nature. While some online communities have a clear leader or coordinator, the life and success of the community depends upon the ownership and contribution of everyone.

Interestingly, each community has unique traits and norms that emerge over time. What is successful in one might not be in another. The people in the community must develop a shared set of norms and values. To join the community, you must learn these norms, even if they are not explicitly stated. If you do not, the community will almost certainly let you know by its silence or even direct chastisement.

Some of these communities last for decades while others exist for only days. New and vibrant online communities develop every day as others turn into Internet ghost towns. The communities thrive as long as their members are involved, value them, and contribute to them.

The world of online networks and communities is an incredibly fluid phenomenon, far more so than what we see in the physical world. It is also far more varied. If you live in a major city, you can find many informal and grassroots networks and communities. They change all the time. Yet, the digital world of communities makes these physical communities look like longstanding establishments.

In Mizuko Ito's book *Hanging Out, Messing Around, and Geeking Out*, she reports on her study of the nature of online connections, particularly with teenagers. She explains at least three distinct types of connections and communities among young people, as articulated in the title of the book.

1. "Hanging out" refers to young people using digital tools to have more lighthearted connections with peers, often serving as an extension of their friendships in the physical world. A group of school friends stays in contact through one or more social media outlets, for example. The driver for this type of online connection is friendship.

2. "Messing around" is different. Ito says this is where young people browse the web, experiment, and play. This activity might be as simple as using a search engine to ask questions and explore ideas of personal interest. The experimentation and play that comes with this might be editing images, creating personal music playlists, customizing their backgrounds on their social media pages, and similar activities.

3. "Geeking out" involves a higher level of focus and commitment to a specific interest. This might mean getting involved with fan-fiction writing, creating and editing videos, learning to program and modify video games, or immersion in a particular video game and its community.

Ito's description is a helpful way to categorize the types of activities that characterize youth involvement online, but it describes the activities of many adults as well.[36]

---

36   Mizuko Ito et al., *Hanging Out, Messing Around, and Geeking Out: Kids Living and Learning with New Media* (Cambridge, MA: MIT Press, 2013).

When I speak to people about the Internet, some say they believe the Internet is mainly about technology or content. But when we examine how most people use it today, the Internet is more about people and connections than about content or specific technologies. Some readers are so immersed in this reality that such a statement seems unnecessary, but there are still others who do not think about the Internet mainly in terms of connecting with people.

Sometimes when I present on the topic, I show an image of a large public swimming pool full of people. There are people of all ages—children playing games, adults playing with infants, a few people trying to avoid the busyness by staying on the edges, and others just soaking and talking with one another. I ask people to tell me what they see. In almost a decade of showing that image, not a single person has told me that they see an interesting technology called a swimming pool. Nobody muses aloud about its construction and design. Instead, they remark on the people in the pool. I suggest that this photo offers a helpful understanding of the digital world today. The Internet is about connecting people, resources, and communities in different ways.

Of course, these connections can have positive and negative effects, which is an important aspect of the digital culture. As a way to illustrate this, consider how the digital world is a place we can witness what Howard Rheingold, an expert on modern communication technology, calls "smart mobs"[37] as well as what some might call "pools of ignorance."

A smart mob, something that can be used for good or ill, consists of a group of people, sometimes even dispersed around the world, using their shared connection and computing power to accomplish something together. There are examples of people coming together online around some social movement, whether it be a protest or to document some sort of civic unrest. Already back in 2006, there were examples of creative uses of such smart mobs to accomplish shared goals; one article labeled this use as "shopping affronts."[38] A shopping affront is when a group of people connect online and agree to meet at a specific store, leveraging their numbers to negotiate a better price. Imagine five hundred or more people showing up at the same store, watching a certain product or set of products. They agree to purchase something if the store manager will give them a special discount.

People are constantly coming up with new ways to leverage connectivity to ac-

---

37 Howard Rheingold, *Smart Mobs: The Next Social Revolution* (Cambridge, MA: Basic Books, 2008).

38 "Shop Affronts," *The Economist*, July 01, 2006, http://www.economist.com/node/7121669#print?story_id=7121669 (accessed March 19, 2017).

complish goals, solve problems, and sometimes just engage in playful banter. A single person or organization does not necessarily run these smart mobs. They can grow organically amid various social media outlets or any place where people connect and collaborate online. Sometimes there is a single instigator, but other times it is difficult to tell how the idea emerged.

Even beyond the smart mob, people online are capable of creating meaningful outcomes without intending to. At one time, Google offered "Google Flu Trends" to track the spread of the flu by location. By tracking the terms people searched—for example, "flu symptoms," "how to treat the flu," "when to go to the doctor with the flu"—the organizers were able to identify flu outbreaks. That is fascinating given that people were not even aware that their actions were contributing to such a collective outcome.[39]

Google Flu Trends is no longer in operation; and actually it failed in some ways. Yet, there are other examples of people contributing to something larger without even realizing they're doing it. reCAPTCHA, first released in 2007, is a technology used to verify that a person is indeed human when filling out an online form. If you have ever filled out a form on a web page and there was a picture of strange or oddly shaped letters you had to type into a box, you experienced reCAPTCHA or one of the offshoots of this technology. What many do not realize is that these pictures with letters come from digital images of real historical documents. Each time you type the letters, you are contributing to digitizing historical documents and making them searchable online. The creators of reCAPTCHA brilliantly addressed two problems at once: They created a tool that confirms that a real person is filling out the form (not a computer or bot scouring the web), and they created a tool that helps to make historical documents searchable on the web.

Of course, all communities and connections online are not necessarily positive ones. In my earlier days of investigating the nature of online community, I came across a particularly troubling site. It was what people call a pro-ana site. Such sites continue to be readily available today, glamorizing and celebrating anorexia as an alternative lifestyle. You can find poems written to the goddess "Ana," tips for purging, graphic images, and more.

There are websites dedicated to helping people cheat on their spouses, engage in sexual promiscuity, engage in illegal activities, share and celebrate pornography, network around racist and other extremist ideals, and much more. There is an ever-growing

---

39 David Lazer and Ryan Kennedy, "What We Can Learn From the Epic Failure of Google Flu Trends," *Wired*, October 1, 2015, https://www.wired.com/2015/10/can-learn-epic-failure-google-flu-trends/ (accessed March 19, 2017).

number of online communities and networks related to any religious expression. Regardless of the topic of interest, people can find one another and assemble online. For those familiar with the Old Testament, these efforts may seem to represent a modern, digital Tower of Babel, with people gathering from around the world and collaborating, but toward less than positive ends.

At the same time, it would be a mischaracterization to claim that this is the only form of connection and collaboration on the web; there are countless positive examples and web services to support them. There are websites created that make it easy to financially support, pray for, and encourage people who are going through health challenges. There are online communities for people to help one another grow and be effective in their various vocations. There are many active Christian ministries using the power and connectivity of the digital world to accomplish their distinct mission or social ministry and direct evangelistic efforts.

Some people are more drawn to exploring how to make good use of these connections and communities than others, which is an important aspect of living in the digital age. The web offers so much more than social media, video sharing, entertainment, news, and free encyclopedias. It is a genuine place where people connect, network, and accomplish shared goals, where they challenge and confront others or find something they are not getting in the physical world. As we think about our role as the Church in this digital age, it is important that we think about how we live out our mission not only in the physical world but also in online contexts.

DISCUSSION AND REFLECTION QUESTIONS

- What role do online communities play in different aspects of your life? If they are a big part of your life, how did they become so? If they are not, what prevents you from engaging with such communities?

- In light of Mizuko Ito's categories, do you find yourself using the web more to "hang out," "mess around," "geek out," or none of the above? If you are discussing this with others, consider sharing one or more examples.

- How does the Internet and digital world at large influence the way you think about connecting with other people? Do you generally think of being connected with people on the Internet as a force for good, ill, or a combination of the two?

WHO ARE THE INTERNET CELEBRITIES TO YOU?

Who are the people you admire or turn to for entertainment, insights, and information online? Are there certain personalities who capture your attention? Why? To what extent do you consider these people positive examples and role models? Consider asking this question to friends and family members. This is a great opportunity to consider the ways in which people in the digital world are influencing us in positive or negative ways.

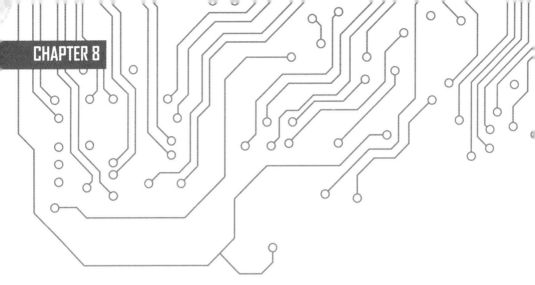

CHAPTER 8

Celebrity Is One Click Away

Anyone with an Internet connection can garner the attention of dozens, hundreds, thousands, even millions of people. Teenagers can create low-budget videos in the family living room and build a following of thousands from around the world. YouTube and its alternatives have become a new route to fame for aspiring singers, musicians, dancers, and other performers. This is a relatively new aspect of life that people did not experience prior to the Internet. YouTube is just one of many such possibilities. There are also blog sites, as mentioned previously. Social media apps allow people to share images and videos, stream live video, host their own shows, and share podcasts.

Through these media, made possible by the Internet, people gather massive followings that they can turn into successful businesses by selling products and services. Some of these people are celebrities who capitalize on their name recognition. But for every celebrity, there are many others who make a name for themselves in one or more of these online forums.

In such a landscape, the digital world becomes yet one more place where we can think about the idea of celebrity and popularity. We may find our worth in the number of people who like, share, value, listen to, watch, or read what we have to say publicly. We find affirmation in looking at our growing number of friends, followers, viewers, and subscribers. When those numbers decline, we might brush it off as not a big deal or we might experience feelings of loss or disappointment.

While new avenues for celebrity are a possibility in this connected age, these technologies are also more broadly about being known and knowing others. In a connected world, you can more easily have your closest connections with people who are thousands of miles away. You might receive encouragement and affirmation of your work from people far away while those in your community know little or nothing about you.

If we are not happy with our friends or connections in the physical world, or if we are too shy or uncomfortable building face-to-face connections, the digital world becomes a supplement or even a replacement for physical interpersonal interaction. Alternatively, some people have great friendships and family connections in the physical world, but they also want to build new and different connections online. People disagree over the value and level of intimacy and true friendship that we might be able to develop in a digital environment, but it is undeniable that connections are happening in such a context.

When I started teaching middle school in the 1990s, this sort of activity was just beginning. Each year I asked my students a few questions about their online activity. In the first year, 1994, perhaps five out of one hundred students reported having a best or close friend online whom they had never met in person. By 2000, that number grew to more like forty in one hundred. The same thing is true for people who met their spouse online. In the earlier days of online dating, some people thought it was unusual. In a matter of a decade, it became a much more commonplace experience. In fact, if you are reading this book with a group of people, it is almost certain that someone in the group has firsthand experience or friends and family members who met their significant others online.

Consider an experience I had when publishing my third book, *What Really Matters? Ten Critical Issues in Contemporary Education*. When the book was first released, the publisher notified me that it was available on the publisher's website and that it would be for sale soon on Amazon.com and other places. I received my complimentary copies in the mail. Only three days later, I received an invitation for an interview on a national radio show. Note that the book was not yet widely available, and the publisher had done a press release but no other marketing up to that point. I had posted a Tweet, an announcement to my Facebook friends, and an entry about the book on my blog. I was surprised to receive an invitation for a radio interview so soon because the word hadn't really gotten out. What surprised me more was that it was not a local radio show. It was not even a radio show in the United States. The request came from a national Christian radio show in New Zealand, literally on the other side of the world from where I lived at the time. I agreed to the interview, which means there were Christians throughout New Zealand who learned about my book before some of my colleagues in my immediate professional networks.

When authors publish their books, they share their ideas with anyone in the world who might happen to read them. Writing in the public sphere has long been a powerful tool for connecting with people. I share my example because of how rapid and far-reaching this connection was. It illustrates that life in a connected world has decreased the limitations of proximity and created ways to build meaningful and mutually beneficially connections with people and groups anywhere in the world.

That is a small personal example, but there are countless other examples of this phenomena of online celebrity or gaining broad attention. There are people who gained celebrity status because of a funny YouTube video they posted. Others found themselves recognized around the world for images that went viral online, sometimes putting them in a favorable light and other times making them objects of laughter or ridicule. Still others, by consistently writing short articles on their personal blogs about areas of personal interest, found themselves with large followings and sometimes even large paychecks from their efforts.

For a growing number, these worldwide digital connections have become a valued and valuable part of business opportunities. Still others use the Internet to build meaningful and valued personal connections with people. To some extent, we all want to be known and appreciated for our work, and the connected world is changing the way that looks for many people. This leads us to the next chapter, where we will further explore the role of connection in an increasingly digital world.

DISCUSSION AND REFLECTION QUESTIONS

- How have you experienced the digital world changing the nature of celebrity, recognition, and influence in your own life or among your friends and colleagues?

- Do you have direct experience with people who have built an audience or made connections with others in ways that would have been difficult prior to the Internet?

- We seem to have a persistent desire to be known, recognized, or valued. Why do you think that is? Can you identify any Bible passages that speak to this?

HOW DO DIGITAL CONNECTIONS MAKE YOU FEEL?

In this chapter, we look at the ways in which connection has become a value, something that many people associate with safety. However, as Christians, there is obviously a far more significant connection in our lives—namely, our connection with God in Jesus Christ. If digital connections give many people a sense of safety, how does this connection that God created with you in your Baptism affect your beliefs as well as your sense of safety, security, and identity?

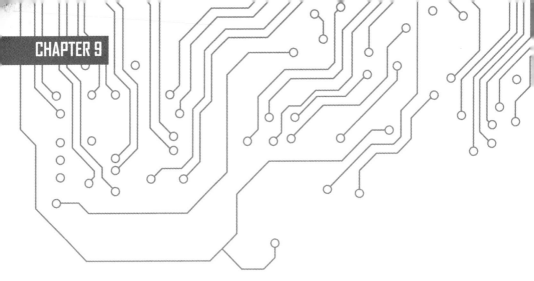

CHAPTER 9

Being Connected Is a Value

In the 1990s, we started to become concerned about the use of cell phones in schools. As more young people brought their phones to school, both teachers and administrators became concerned about misuse and the distractions associated with these devices. So schools began to develop policies about cell phones. At first, we saw quite a few schools ban cell phones entirely. But over time, schools relaxed the requirements, allowing students to bring cell phones to school only if the phones remained in lockers during the day. Then some schools started to allow students to carry their phones with them all the time, though there were still rules about keeping phones turned off. Eventually the rules changed again. Now phones could be on but needed to be in silent mode or turned off during exams. These adjustments continue today, when we find teachers designing lessons that use students' cell phones as part of the classroom experience.

Of course, not all teachers are designing lessons that make use of cell phones; but this progression reflects an important pattern of life in the digital world. This evolution of policies and practices about cell phone use points to the changing nature of a technology in society and in the school environment as well. These changes emerge as more people became comfortable with the role of a given technology. There are still plenty of schools with strict rules about cell phones, but we have now reached a point when more and more people have increasingly come to see cell phones as necessary resources we are inherently entitled to.

This is not just a technological change; it is a social and potentially psychological change as well. People's thinking and attitudes about the role and acceptability of cell phones changed, and that influenced policies. Consider the following informal survey that I conducted over a number of years. When I had the opportunity groups of people ranging in age, I asked a simple question: How would you .. a cross-country drive without a cell phone? Consistently, older people seemed more comfortable with such a prospect. Younger people, however, often expressed various levels of anxiety about the idea. When I asked them to explain their anxiety, they said that the cell phone is a means of connection with other people. "What would I do if I had a flat tire or if someone needed to contact me?"

The cell phone has become, for many, a means of connection with people and re-sources that make us feel safer and more secure. Parents buy phones for their children so they can stay in near-constant contact via text, call, or app, and this has become the new normal in terms of staying connected. People constantly check their social media messages, texts, and email to stay as connected as possible. Various studies remind us of the amazing number of times that many of us check our phones for messages through-out the day. Once source claims that the average smartphone user touches the device more than twenty-five hundred times a day.[40]

Old telephone commercials used to promote the traditional phone service by say-ing, "Reach out and touch someone."[41] That is not enough for many people today. To-day, many of us value staying in touch with multiple people twenty-four hours a day and seven days a week. Constant connectivity is a growing assumption about the nature of life in the contemporary world, for better or for worse.

Because I write and think about these things, I thought myself immune to this concept of constant connectivity. I discovered that I'm not. A few years ago, my in-laws purchased a summer home in the Upper Peninsula of Michigan. It is beautiful little home on a quiet lake, with a wall of windows looking out toward the water. While not actually true, I often joke that it is a place where there are more bears than people. It is quiet, serene, and beautiful. After a hectic week at work, one would think that driving to this home and settling in would offer relief and relaxation. That is what I expected. When I arrived there the first time, I carried my bags to my room, and then went out to enjoy the view of the lake. It was stunning. After a few minutes, out of habit, I checked my phone for emails, only to find that there was no cell coverage—not a single bar. I am a little embarrassed to admit that I experienced actual panic in that moment. My mind filled with "what if" scenarios. The closest hospital is almost forty-five minutes by car,

40   "We Touch Our Phones 2,617 Times a Day, Says Study," Network World, July 7, 2016, http://www.networkworld.com/article/3092446/smartphones/we-touch-our-phones-2617-times-a-day-says-study.html (accessed July 9, 2017).

41   CulturalLag, "AT&T Reach Out and Touch Someone Commercial—1987," YouTube, March 13, 2014, https://www.youtube.com/watch?v=OapWdclVqEY (accessed March 19, 2017).

so what if someone became sick, got injured, or had an allergic reaction? How could we contact emergency services to send a helicopter for rescue? Most of my anxieties revolved around the thought that we had no landline or other means of connecting with outside help if we needed it. What I expected to be a time of relaxation quickly turned into near panic.

How did people manage to survive all those centuries without cell phones? Did they live in constant panic about "what if" moments? These questions are not just about cell phone service; they speak to our larger reliance upon the services and resources that many of us expect in modern life. Yet, because of my research of this topic over the years, I am convinced that the cell phone is the main cause of this new priority and value for constant and instant connectivity. The growth and adoption of this technology led to the development of these emotional connections.

It is not just cell phones connecting us to emergency services. These devices allow us to maintain connections with specific and important people in our lives as well. As a high school teacher, I had more than one parent insist that his or her child be able to keep a cell phone on at all times in case the parent needed to contact the child. The thought of not having immediate and direct contact was intolerable.

All of this represents a dominant value in the digital age. Connectivity is not simply something that is nice to have in our lives. It is a priority and a value, one that affects many aspects of our lives, even our sense of safety and security. We can make an argument that these connections do make us safer and more secure. As parents, we can stay more informed about our children, where they are, what they are doing, and whether they are okay. In cases of emergency or an unexpected event, such as a flat tire, it is far easier to get help when you have a cell phone—and service. At the same time, there are some limitations to this value of connectivity. We sometimes depend upon working technology to be at peace, or at least at ease, in a situation, but we might find ourselves distracted from what is in front of us. It could be that this elevated value of digital connection sometimes prevents us from building stronger connections with the people around us at the moment when we choose a text conversation with a remote friend rather than a friendly discussion with a stranger in the grocery store line, while sitting in the airport, or even at dinner with family. As with every topic in this book, there are benefits and limitations, which is why we are wise to use this as an opportunity to consider the implications of the connected life and how we can make decisions that demonstrate our beliefs and values.

DISCUSSION AND REFLECTION QUESTIONS

- How important for you is being digitally connected? How important is it for the people around you?

- In what ways do you see technology changing people's sense of safety?

- What thoughts or feelings do you experience when you are not digitally connected? Does it cause you to feel anxious, relaxed, peaceful, or something else?

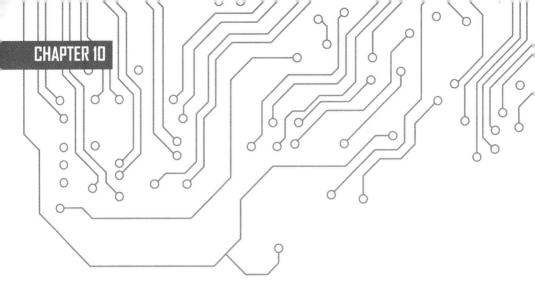

CHAPTER 10

A War between Democratizing
and Authoritarian Technology

Consider the differences between two sources of power: wind and nuclear. Both have the same end use, but there are many differences between them. A farm of windmills is governed by rules and regulations and requires approvals from the local, state, and federal agencies. But the rules and regulations for windmills number far fewer compared to those for a nuclear power plant. The reason is obvious. The dangers and risks associated with nuclear power are far greater than those associated with wind power. Therefore, the government regulates one more than the other. One has tall fences, guard shacks, complex security systems, and people guarding it. The other is located in large, open fields with little to nothing preventing people from walking right up to them. This type of distinction between wind and nuclear power innovations applies to many other technologies in the modern world as well.

Some distinguish between these two types of emerging technologies as authoritarian and democratizing.[42] The democratizing technologies, such as the windmill, are those that appear to empower individuals. These technologies are available to the vast majority of people, and while there might be some regulation, there is limited centralized control over the technologies. Sometimes people try to control democratizing technologies, but such technologies usually find a way to empower individuals despite the best efforts of specific groups or individuals. You know that it is a democratizing

---

42 Lewis Mumford, "Authoritarian and Democratic Technics," *Technology and Culture* 5 (Winter 1964): 1–8.

technology because you will often see hobbyists and self-taught people use it and have interest in it.

Authoritarian technologies, by nature, call for more centralized control and protection. The use, cost, complexity, and safety issues associated with these technologies drive people to accept centralized control and restricted access to them. Most people agree with protecting and securing authoritarian technology for the good of the whole.

It is not always clear to us whether a technology is democratizing or authoritarian. However, we usually notice them by the politics surrounding them, the regulations that people tend to accept or reject, and the extent to which we see grassroots innovators working with the technologies. Let us consider a few examples.

Is the Internet an authoritarian or democratizing technology? In its earliest days, the Internet was made up of a small group of people who used computer networks to connect and communicate. A core group of people controlled it. Yet, it did not take long for this to expand. The fact that a tech-minded person could build a local, physical network of computers (LAN, or local area network) or connect to a broader network of computers (WAN, or wide area network)—which eventually became a web of networks (WWW, or the World Wide Web)—shows the Internet's largely democratizing nature. There are people who continue to argue for greater centralized control and regulation, but much of the Internet as we know it remains open and welcoming of grassroots efforts. It does not take much to build a web presence, connect with countless groups or individuals, and leverage the technology to build a solid business in the digital space.

There are, of course, certain groups that have far more control and power than others. There are behemoth companies and organizations on the web. There are the people who are powerful and widespread influencers on the Internet. Alongside them are twelve-year-old hobbyists who are leaving their mark and taking advantage of the Internet to accomplish their goals and explore their interests. If you have enough money for a device and an Internet connection, or if you have transportation to a public library, you can benefit from the mass collection of data, connections, and resources via the Internet. You can consume information, and you can create it. You can learn, champion for your favorite causes, gain valued information, and so much more.

What about social media? This is one of many aspects of the Internet as we think of it today, and the interests and actions of the users drive social media sites. A service such as Facebook has rules and systems in place that influence what we do and restrict what we can post. At the same time, users have significant leeway with what they post, how they post it, and where they post it. Users decide whom they friend and whom they unfriend or block. Users create the content that other users consume. The same thing is true for other social sites, such as Instagram, Pinterest, Twitter, Snapchat, and the like. Each of these services has unique rules and restrictions. The question is whether such services are democratizing, meaning that they amplify the freedom and choices of the users, or authoritarian, meaning that users are more closely policed and monitored.

We can ask this question about any technology, but the answer is not always clear. Sometimes technologies empower the individual but use subtle or direct ways to control and influence. Most of us think of social media and the Internet as democratizing. The opportunity to build connections, access information, and contribute content is increasingly available to the majority of people in the developed world. Having access to social media provides opportunities that are not otherwise be available.

In fact, not having access to the Internet today can decrease one's voice and opportunities. How do you even find out about the breadth of job opportunities or apply for a job without Internet access? How do you search for consumer safety information and recalls for products that you purchased? How do you investigate the position of political candidates when the debates do not fully reveal their positions? How do you access the best health information and search for the best specialist? What if you want to learn something new, from fixing your own lawn mower to starting a new business?

Arguably, those who have Internet access are at an advantage over those who do not. While we acknowledge that information does not equate with wisdom, information is nonetheless critical for many aspects of our daily lives. Internet access is not just about access to information, however. As we examined in the chapter about celebrity, there is also a democratization of how we communicate what we say to other people. Also, more than any time in history, almost any willing person can share ideas and information with the rest of the world. Some might argue that this is creating a mass of low quality content, but it is also offering massive numbers of people a forum for their ideas.

This idea became so central in the early years of this century that when *Time* magazine announced its annual person of the year in 2006, something unusual occurred. In most years, *Time* magazine uses the cover of this issue to recognize a person of great influence in the world: a political leader, a humanitarian, or sometimes a respected or accomplished athlete. None of these made the cover in 2006. Instead, *Time* announced that "You" are the person of the year.[43] Intending to recognize the user-centered and participatory nature of the web, *Time* magazine's editors used this issue to celebrate the

---

43   "Person of the Year 2006," *Time* magazine, http://content.time.com/time/specials/packages/0,28757,2019341,00.html (accessed March 19, 2017).

countless and sometimes unknown people who voluntarily write and edit Wikipedia articles. They recognized those creating blogs on thousands of topics, freely sharing their thoughts or ideas. They included the ever-growing volume of videos uploaded to YouTube, the many people who started their own podcasts, the members of thousands of online communities, those using social media, those contributing reviews of products, and much more. *Time* recognized the power of the individual in this new digital age.

We especially see this power at work in social media. At its worst, we see heated political debates among friends, family members, and complete strangers that seem more divisive than helpful. We also witness people using this freedom of expression to bully or ridicule others. At its best, people use it to offer useful information, encourage one another, and build one another up. Either way, it is helpful to consider how both democratizing and authoritarian technologies influence us.

An important question that we will examine in the second part of this book relates to how we use the freedom and influence available to us today. Will we use it to encourage others and build others up? Will we use it to spread divisiveness and dissension? The Ten Commandments apply to all aspects of our lives, and that includes our increasingly digital lives, but it is easy for us to compartmentalize, especially in the digital world.

DISCUSSION AND REFLECTION QUESTIONS

- Think of the technologies that most influence your life. Do you view them as primarily democratizing or authoritarian? Explain.

- Social media gives a greater number of people the ability to share ideas and resources with others. What do you see as the benefits and the limitations of this?

- In this chapter, we looked at how not having Internet access might put people at a disadvantage compared to others. Have you seen or experienced examples of this? What are some potential benefits to having less Internet access?

WHAT CAN A ROBOT DO FOR YOU?

As we explore what might sound like science fiction to some readers, I invite you to think about your own thoughts and comfort level with robots and the roles they play (or could play) in your life. What are parts of your life or work where you could see robots doing good, where you are more comfortable with their use? What are parts of your life or the life of your family members where you would be concerned about the use of robots? See if you can surface some of the reasons for your answers to these last two questions. How do you determine the appropriate use in different contexts? Can you think of any Scripture passages that might guide your thoughts and decisions on this matter?

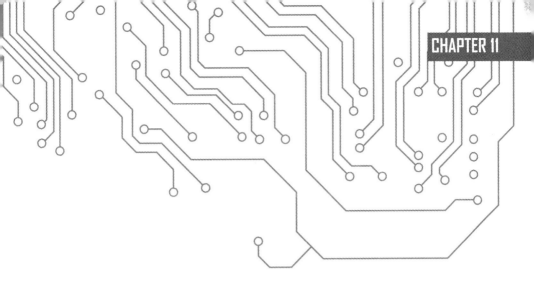

CHAPTER 11

Robots and the Future of Work and Life

While many of the topics so far relate to the Internet and related technologies, the digital world is finding its way into our lives in a myriad of ways. There is growing interest in how digital and technological advancements will influence the nature of work and all aspects of life. What I describe in this chapter might sound like something out of the Jetsons[44] or some more contemporary depiction of a futuristic world, but we are getting closer to that world every day, especially in terms of how robotics continue to change the type and nature of work and life.

There is a risk to writing too much about such a rapidly developing topic because anything I write now will undoubtedly become increasingly outdated. However, this topic represents an important enough shift that I consider it worth the risk. Consider this short list of changes underway:

- It is quite likely that driverless cars will replace many truck drivers, bus drivers, and taxi drivers. Driverless cars will be commonplace in our communities.

- Factories have switched and continue to switch from humans to robots on some assembly lines. This does not necessarily mean that all jobs will be lost; people will be working alongside robots.

---

44 This is a reference to a cartoon show that was short-lived in the 1960s and then showed up again in the 1980s. The show was about a family living far in the future. It was a sort of futuristic take on another show, the Flintstones, which followed a family in prehistoric times. The life of the Jetsons was one of fly cars, holograms, robots, and countless contraptions that shaped their daily life and work.

- Even as some worry about the lack of people to fill jobs in certain fields (such as healthcare), others are turning to robots to eventually replace some of the tasks currently completed by doctors and other healthcare workers.[45]

- Computers are being designed that can write new computer programs, potentially doing work that previously required a human computer programmer.

- Computer-aided technologies continue to drive strong debate about the teacher per student ratio necessary in classrooms, with some arguing (albeit quite controversially) that we will be able to decrease the number of teachers needed for a class of students.

- The drive toward analytics and data-driven decisions further solidifies the possibility of computerized solutions for tasks like advising college students, monitoring progress toward company goals, or identifying pressing problems in organizations.

- Research in almost every field is looking at ways to reduce the human labor cost by replacing a percentage of the workforce with increasingly sophisticated and complex computerized and robotic solutions.

- While we once left the idea of a cyborg existence to science fiction, there are real-world applications in healthcare and beyond. This combination of the human and technological ranges from prosthetics for amputees to far more experimental research around technological enhancements to the human brain.

- Researchers are showing that younger generations are increasingly comfortable replacing a human connection with a computerized or computer-mediated connection, at least for common tasks like checking out at the grocery store and banking. More controversially, as mentioned in an earlier chapter, there are also experiments in replacing human companionship with a technological equivalent, supplement, or substitute.

These possibilities may conjure images of movies like *The Terminator* or *Trans-*

---

45 Joelle Renstrom, "Robot Nurses Will Make Shortages Obsolete," *The Daily Beast*, September 24, 2016, http://www.thedailybeast.com/articles/2016/09/24/robot-nurses-will-make-shortages-obsolete.html (accessed March 19, 2017).

formers, where intelligent robots surpass human intelligence and seek to take over the world. The jury is out on that one, but all of these changes have more than a few implications for our beliefs and convictions. At a minimum, countless people will find themselves out of work or needing training for a new line of work. This is significant, but this is not the first time people have faced such challenges.

Perhaps you have heard someone use the word *Luddite* to describe another person. Alternatively, maybe you have heard someone sheepishly (or proudly) self-identify as one. The modern meaning is a person who is skeptical or critical of the alleged promise and benefits of one or more modern technologies, but that is not the entire story. Its original use was in a historical context that involved more than just skepticism or criticism.

The term originally comes from the early nineteenth century when new technologies replaced and displaced workers in the textile mills in England. Owners of the mills determined that these machines were a justifiable improvement upon what the workers were able to do. Angry and uncertain about their futures, some of the workers started a revolt. Led by a fictional or mythical character whom people called Ned Ludd, some of these workers broke into mills, destroying the machines that threatened their livelihood.

In other words, the original Luddites were not just skeptics or even outspoken critics. They were people who were willing to break the law and even vandalize to be heard or to try to reverse the course of technological developments that jeopardized their way of life. They were rebels and activists fueled by the negative personal impact of new technologies.

Today, those who embrace the label of Luddite are far less likely to take such an approach. Instead, they are usually people who resist the use of emerging technologies in their personal lives and, to an extent, in their work lives; or perhaps they are outspoken about their dislike of technological development (usually limited to certain domains that conflict with certain values). Most Luddites today are quite happy with advancements in medical technology. They might enjoy the benefits of modern transportation technology. They live in homes supported by a variety of modern heating and cooling technologies. They benefit from advancement in sanitation technologies in their communities. Yet there are some areas where they believe technology undermines their preferred way of life. For example, they do not appreciate being told their jobs are on the line if they refuse to learn to use modern technologies. This applies to almost every industry today.

There are, of course, people today whose experiences parallel the plight of the first Luddites because new technology is likely to replace their jobs. In this age of robotics and automated tasks, our broader conversations about workforce development must take into account the fact that we will continue to see jobs eliminated, replaced, or at a minimum, augmented and changed by technology.

Yet we can learn from the experiences of the original Luddites. One important lesson is that they failed. Their revolt did not save their jobs. It did not prevent machines from replacing them. It did not slow technological development in their society or industry. The same thing is true today.

That does not mean, though, that we cannot speak up and strive to shape the ways we use technology. In fact, I contend that we have a moral obligation to do so. It does also mean that we must recognize that we are moving quickly into a future where the man versus machine dichotomy (or synergy) will become increasingly common. The nature of work is changing, and we are wise to have serious and candid conversations about what this means for education, society, families, and the workforce.

What do we, as Christians and as a Church, have to say about this? Coming from a Lutheran tradition, I hold dear the doctrine of vocation, which teaches that all good work is a means of love for neighbor. Or as others prefer to explain it, we serve as masks of God as He shares His good gifts to others through our work.[46] What happens, then, when a growing number of people find their good work replaced by robotic and mechanistic replacements? As people worry about putting food on the table for their families and finding ways to be active and contributing members of society, the Church still has an important message to share. We have an opportunity to, once more, remind people that their worth and identity does not come from a specific task or job but in God's love for us in Christ. The Church may find itself in a position to assist a growing number of people amid job transitions, helping them to see both their worth and their continued calling to love of neighbor, even if the nature of their employment changes over time.

Another aspect of this shift toward the robotic and the mechanized is that some will lament what appears to be a dehumanizing of daily activities. For example, in some stores, I no longer greet the person at the cash register, share a few kind words, and count out money. I just insert a card at the self-checkout. Perhaps I skip the physical store altogether and order everything I need from the comfort of my own home, with a few clicks on my phone or computer or a voice command to my smart speaker. How is all of this affecting our opportunity to engage in genuine human interactions?

This brings us back to a topic discussed at the beginning of the book. As our in-

46   AE 14:114.

teractions with the mechanistic and robotic continue to expand, we will certainly find more people asking fundamental questions about what it means to be human. What makes a human different from a robot or a machine? As people personify the technology in their lives, what are the implications of people turning to technology to address needs previously met by humans?

Some might delight in their robot vacuum cleaners, saving them from a task they did not enjoy. Yet even robot vacuums are expanding; companies are building robot nannies to care for children and the elderly. Already in 2015, SoftBank, a Japanese company, put a robot on the market to address a shortage of nannies.[47] Their solution was a robot that reads and responds to human emotions. The company offers this as a solution for childcare and for healthcare assistance for the elderly. There will certainly be expanded applications of this kind of technology in the future as we are already seeing robot solutions focus upon service and caregiving, not just replacing people in factory assembly lines.

All such innovations lead us to rely more on machines and less on people. Some of us look at such changes with concern, wondering how this might diminish much-needed human interaction.

There are many questions to explore, but I remain hesitant to offer too definitive answers on these matters. I do maintain, however, that the Church has an important role in these changes. We have a voice in the conversation about what it means to be human, the nature of authentic community and human relationships, the worth of the individual, the value of the doctrine of vocation, and what God's Word says about all of it. We can be a place where people are welcome to ask difficult questions, grapple with the significant implications of these changes, discover answers in God's Word, and ultimately find solace and strength at the foot of the cross when everything else is changing.

---

47   Lucy Ingham and Daniel Davies, "Robot nanny to be sold in Japanese stores from 2015," *Factor*, January 7, 2015, http://factor-tech.com/robotics/4301-robot-nanny-to-be-sold-in-japanese-stores-from-2015/ (accessed March 19, 2017).

DISCUSSION AND REFLECTION QUESTIONS

- Some of the ideas in this chapter may sound more like science fiction than reality. Can you list any examples from your life of robotics replacing people or human connections?

- Mentally walk through your typical week, scanning your various activities. How many of those activities are human-technology exchanges that would have been human-to-human interactions in the past? Consider exploring this question with people from other generations for even more interesting insights.

- How do you see technology shaping the way people think about the purpose and nature of their work? Do you see it influencing their sense of worth or value in the workplace?

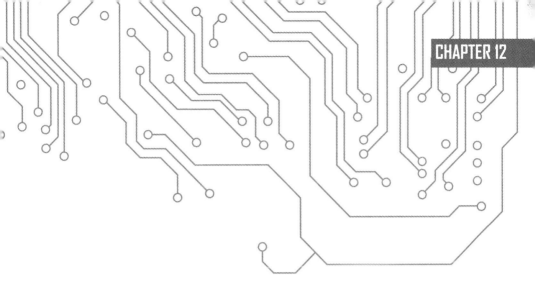

CHAPTER 12

Technology as Messiah?

Think of how much we depend upon technology in our daily lives. We rely upon it to heat, cool, clean, and give light in our homes and workplaces, prepare our foods, and keep our cars in good working order. We rely upon it to stay in touch with friends, relatives, and co-workers. We lean on it to help organize our days, tell time, and travel. We use it to help diagnose and treat illness. We have networked homes, churches, schools, workplaces, and communities; and we increasingly rely upon those networks to keep everything running.

In the previous chapters, we explored some of the ways technology is shaping life in the twenty-first century. From changes in acquiring information to communication, technology is an increasingly integrated part of our world—so much so that we do not even think of many of these aspects as technology. They are just part of our lives!

Years ago, when I was working on my doctoral dissertation, I experienced a moment of realization about how much technology was integrated into my own life. I am a runner, and I often use that time to organize my thoughts for my research. Interestingly, my dissertation related to the impact of technology in our lives. As I finished a long run, I paused for a moment to think about the different technologies around me. I had a GPS watch tracking my distance and time. I had an iPod for music. I had a heart-rate monitor strapped around my chest. In that moment, I started to wonder if the idea of a cyborg was not far off. As I walked into my house and over to my computer to record my running time and distance, I passed kitchen gadgets and appliances, a cell phone, a television (or maybe two), and three different computers. I turned on my computer screen to find more than a dozen documents open, each representing a different project. Pondering this, I looked at the very long list of programs on my computer. Nothing that I am describing is earth-shattering or surprising to many readers. This is an increasingly commonplace existence in the twenty-first century.

A major question, however, relates to the priority we place on all of this technology. What is its proper place in our lives? How much do we rely upon it and for what purposes? When confronted with a problem, we turn to one or more technologies to help us solve it. Consequently, a growing number of us have come to lean on various technologies to save us from otherwise unpleasant outcomes or situations. As one friend quipped, "Technology is our guardian angel in the digital world."

Like all tools available to us, technology is a gift we can use for good. We can use it to help heal, teach, provide support, connect, fund important causes, increase awareness about issues, provide good and valuable products and services, and so much more. A hammer in the hand of a humanitarian can turn a person into a Laborer For Christ. A car and a microwave can turn into a meal program for shut-ins. A computer and Internet connection can turn into a remote tutoring program or a hotline for abused women. Technology itself is not doing these things, but it can amplify these worthy and valuable efforts. Sometimes it makes helping possible in ways that were not available before. All of these are good and laudable uses of technology in our digital and connected world, and we will explore these sorts of uses in the second part of this book.

Yet there is another side to this. Just as some might look to the stars and worship them instead of seeing them as the handiwork of the Creator, so we can find ourselves worshiping the technologies that improve the conditions of our lives and extend our capabilities in the world. In this way, if we are not careful, we can find that we have turned modern technology into an idol.

In the First Commandment, God tells us, "You shall have no other gods before Me." Idolatry is not just worshiping deities of other religions. An idol is anything we put in the place that properly belongs only to God. Pascal described it as follows:

> What is it then that this desire and this inability proclaim to us, but that there was once in man a true happiness of which there now remain to him only the mark and empty trace, which he in vain tries to fill from all his surroundings, seeking from things absent the help he does not obtain in things present? But these are all inadequate, because the infinite abyss can only be filled by an infinite and immutable object, that is to say, only by God Himself.[48]

---

48   Blaise Pascal, *Pensées* (Salt Lake City: Project Gutenberg, 2006), April 27, 2006, https://www.gutenberg.org/files/18269/18269-h/18269-h.htm (accessed March 19, 2017).

Proverbs 19:22 reminds us, "What is desired in a man is steadfast love, and a poor man is better than a liar." In other words, each of us craves a certain type of love. We yearn for a love that is unfailing and unconditional. Sometimes that love comes from other people. A husband and wife seek this from each other, but no human is capable of providing unfailing and unconditional love. In fact, expecting it of another person is the futile effort of trying to get perfect love from an imperfect human. If we are not careful, our misplaced search for this kind of love can overwhelm us to the extent that it undermines positive relationships with spouses, other family members, and friends. Who is capable of living up to such a standard? The truth is that the only source of that unfailing, unconditional love is the triune God. It is God's love in Christ that fills this gap, allowing us to approach relationships with others without the burden of unrealistic expectations.

Yet today, people are seeking love and answers to their greatest problems not only from other people; we are also turning to technology. We may come to rely on it as our source of hope and comfort, setting God aside. We see technology as the beacon of light and hope for a better future for us and the rest of the world, believing that it will deliver us from the darkness of disease, disaster, poverty, war, and other troubles in our world and lives. When we seek love, security, healing, solutions to society's most pressing problems, safety, or any other basic need from technologies or the people who wield them, we are tempted to act as if they play the role of messiah—a role that only Jesus properly fills.

This is not to say that technology should not play a role in solving problems. By its very nature, that is the purpose of technology. People invent technologies to solve problems and create opportunities. The incredible medical advancements of our era are undeniable. Surgeries once thought impossible are commonplace. Diseases that once were life-threatening now are cured by medical treatments. Vaccines, devices, and medications are daily improving the quality of people's lives in demonstrable ways.

These same results are true for technology in other parts of our lives as well. Advances have radically improved safety in the workplace and on the highways. Technologies have allowed for cleaner air, water, and soil. They preserve artifacts, keep track of our pets, and teach us the catechism.[49]

The important differences, however, reside in where we see the ultimate solution to our greatest needs and whether we worship the created or the Creator. Technologies

---

49   For example, Concordia Publishing House added Luther's Small Catechism to the Amazon Echo, allowing confirmation students or others to get help from Alexa to practice memory work.

are possible because of the many gifts our gracious God grants to humanity. Just as it is misplaced to worship the stars instead of the God who created them, it is misplaced to stop at merely using technology instead of taking the next steps of repenting of the bad that comes from it and giving all thanks to God for the good it brings.

Technology is simply applied scientific knowledge, and some people use science as a replacement for God or faith. Claims are made that science is superior to religion, that it is more practical and, in essence, can replace the need for God.[50] Science and technology take priority over faith in the God of Scripture in much of the world today, but the persistent search for a savior, a messiah, and perfect love remains. Some see that savior, that greatest hope, in the next great technology. For the Christian, however, there is only one Messiah, and that is Jesus Christ. Technology gives us both the challenge and the opportunity to be faithful, diligent witnesses to this fact.

DISCUSSION AND REFLECTION QUESTIONS

- List at least two examples when you or others were tempted to place hope in technological progress instead of in God.

- Think about how various technologies are advertised and promoted. What basic human needs and desires do these advertisements cater to?

- How do you achieve balance between being grateful for technologies as blessings and gifts from God and trusting technology more than God for what you need each day?

---

50 Deborah Orr, "Science Is My God," *The Guardian*, June 09, 2011, https://www.theguardian.com/science/2011/jun/09/science-is-my-god (accessed March 19, 2017).

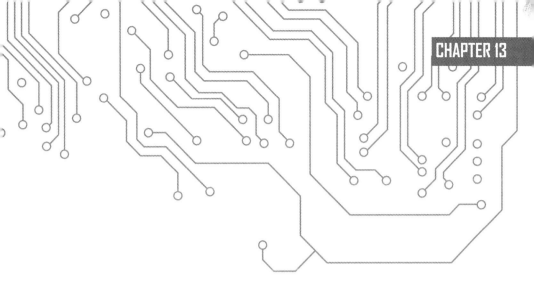

CHAPTER 13

Changing Views in the Digital Age

As the previous chapters illustrated, technology is changing our view on any number of issues. It is changing our views of authority. It is changing the way we think about what it means to be human. It is changing our view of the written word, of truth, of reality. And it is changing our view of religion. As we conclude this first section, which looked at the ways technology influences modern life and thought, consider the subtle and sometimes significant ways our views are changing in some of these areas. I offer a few reflections and summary remarks on some of the major shifts that seem to be part of these many technological developments.

AUTHORITY

There was a time when authority figures were the primary and sometimes only source of information or expertise on a given subject. Your doctor was your source of medical knowledge. Your mechanic was the source of knowledge about your car. Your lawyer was your source of knowledge about legal matters. Your teacher was the primary or core source of information about most subjects (although libraries provided supplemental information). This is changing. While there have always been self-directed learners and others who managed to go beyond the insight offered directly by these experts, learning has changed in significant ways. Knowledge is a mere click away.

A significant side effect to expanding technologies is that people can easily search for answers to questions about everything: health, cars, law, academics, the list goes on. The information available online is not always vetted, nor do the consumers of that information necessarily have the expertise to accurately interpret and apply what they find. Yet, increasingly they do. More people today are gaining the consumer confidence and insight to challenge the experts. Sometimes they do this in error, but other times they do it correctly and to their benefit.

Access to information challenges the status of some of these authority figures. We certainly still value and need doctors, but they hear more doubts and questions from patients than in the past. The same is true for other experts such as pastors and teachers. We are long past the time when pastors and teachers were among the most educated people in most communities. And since individuals can easily find information about the subjects taught by pastors and teachers, more people have the confidence to venture out on their own to explore, learn, and test the words and ideas of one authority figure against another.

The lived experience of a person of authority or expertise today is far different from past decades, and this is likely to continue to change in the upcoming years. The Internet has democratized access to knowledge and information, which has forever changed the way we relate to experts and authority figures. This means that simple appeals to authority may be diminishing in perceived value. Fewer people believe a pastor just because he is a pastor or an expert on theological matters. A growing number of people are skeptical of whether his title means the pastor is right. Perhaps the way of the Bereans is more important than ever. Paul commended them for not trusting him at his words. They examined the Scriptures, testing Paul's words against what they read there. There is great value in doing the same thing in our churches today.

What It Means to Be Human

While the fundamentals of what it means to be human have not changed, life in a technological world influences the way people think about the human experience, human limitations, and even what it means to be human. This is also nothing new. There is a long history of people thinking about life differently because of technology.

Consider the invention of what many think of as a basic technology: eyeglasses. Prior to that invention, there was no solution to poor vision. Poor eyesight was limiting and even crippling. While there are examples of people with complete visual impairment who accomplished great things and enjoyed a high quality of life, limited vision affected how people went about various activities. The technology of corrective lenses helped to overcome limitations and allowed people to engage in some of the same activities as those with perfect vision.

Other technologies did more than address limitations caused by visual impairment—they extended human sight. Both the telescope and the microscope are examples of this. The telescope extends the natural limits of human vision and allows one to see far into the night sky, to see the moon up close and gaze at distant planets. At the opposite end of the scale, the microscope expands the natural limitations of vision by allowing us to see what cannot be seen with the naked eye.

We are using technology to extend our natural human capacities. We amplify ordinary vision by technology. Corrective lenses, telescopes, and microscopes are so familiar that we seldom pause to consider them as innovations.

Living in such an integrated relationship with technology changes the human experience. It is so infused with our ordinary experience that it seems like a natural part of who we are and of the human experience. People with contacts or glasses stop thinking of it as a technology and think of it more as a part of them.

This is not just limited to vision devices, of course. This is widespread in the medical world. There are prosthetics, plates, epoxies, and other technologies used to address damaged bones and joints. There are pacemakers, cochlear implants, and artificial organs. The military uses technologies to amplify natural human strength, allowing one to accomplish tasks not possible for ordinary people.

Most of us think about such innovations in varying levels of extreme. We might be comfortable with eyeglasses and joint replacement, but we look at emerging technologies that promise the amplification of human abilities with concern and suspicion. How much is too much? At what point do we delve into a cyborg future, where we mix the human and the technological so much so that we think of them as one?

While most people do not yet think about such extremes on a daily basis, in some arenas this is a real and growing conversation. Countless researchers, inventors, and investors are exploring technologies that work in concert with the human body. There is even a field of study and growing group of people who are deeply involved in what they refer to as transhumanism. Transhumanists believe that the current state of our physical and mental abilities can evolve, creating new abilities and addressing critical health and other human limitations through integration with technology. They aspire to extend the human lifespan and mental capacities and improve the way we address illnesses such as heart disease, cancer, and cataracts. Some even believe transhumanists will solve the problem of death through scientific and technological means (hence the reason for this last chapter on the growing view of technology as a sort of messiah).

The Written Word

While the written word seems like it has been around forever, even that is a technology that once caused suspicion and concern. Centuries ago, people like Socrates and Plato expressed concern that the written word would dull the mind, taking away from the richness of oral communication.[51] This suspicion certainly was borne out, but communication wasn't hindered. Yet, the written word is not static. It continues to change, perpetually influenced by developments throughout the ages.

Consider the simple but significant example of hypertext, which allows us to turn any word or phrase on a screen into a link that takes us somewhere else. It can take a reader to another word on the same page or to a web page created and hosted on the other side of the world. Hypertext contributed to the widespread growth and use of the World Wide Web.

Hypertext links information and ideas from disparate sources across time and space. This is quite different from text of the past. The closest familiar parallels might be a study Bible with notes that reference other verses or an encyclopedia that references other parts of the encyclopedia yet remains within the same collection. In a collection of encyclopedias, however, the same person might not author it all, but a common organization or entity vetted and organized it. With text on the web, this is no longer true. You can link and mix and match in ways that never existed with text of the past. Instead of fully explaining a statement, you can just create a link to one that is already explained or illustrated. You blend your unique creation with a vast variety of existing creations; you support your ideas and arguments with those of others.

As with all technologies, there are affordances and limitations to hypertext. Its affordances consist of linking disparate sources, creating a new way for sharing information. Its limitations include potentially distracting a reader or taking him or her away from full immersion in a single text by a single author. Of course, different people will offer their concerns and critiques in different ways, but what is certain is that text is changing in the digital world because of hypertext.

Truth

Absolute truth has certainly not changed because of the digital age. What is true for all times, all people, and all places continues to be true. Yet how people seek to discern truth and how they think about it is changing in the digital world.

Because there is so much information available to us today and because the reliability of that information varies substantially from one source to another, there are different ways that people handle this. Some have become completely skeptical of anything that claims to be true. Instead of persisting in trying to discern what is true and what is not, some dismiss truth altogether. "With the right software and videography skills, you can make anything seem true," they argue. Some people are more open to

51   Plato, *The Dialogues of Plato,* trans. Benjamin Jowett (Oxford: Clarendon Press, 1969), 275–77.

believing truth claims. Others respond differently, closing themselves off to other truth claims. They limit themselves to select sources of information and label everything else as suspect or even wrong.

These are not the only responses, of course, but the sheer wealth of information is such that we stop taking the time to analyze the claims with care. Even the most analytical among us can fall into this trap. We see this at work especially on social media. A friend, colleague, or family member posts a link to some article about a startling fact or bit of news only to discover that it is a spoof—fake news. A vivid visual makes this even more deceptive. A well-educated and intelligent colleague once posted an image on social media that showed a group of high-school-age kids sitting on a bench in a museum. There was a large, beautiful Rembrandt painting on the wall behind them, but they all stared at their phones. My colleague posted this as evidence of how technology is hurting young people and of the distorted nature of life in this technological world. Yet that photograph has more than one interpretation. It turns out that it depicts a group of students on a field trip. The teacher assigned the tasks of using the museum app to do research on art they saw. The students were actually engaged in work assigned by their teacher. There was another photo showing them looking intently at art with their phones nowhere in sight. We can all fall into this trap; truth calls for discernment.

Some of us persist in striving to discern truth from falsehood, but it is a time-consuming task. We only have so many hours in the day, and if we do not intentionally manage the influx of information, it is impossible to be thoughtful and analytical. We must somehow learn to prioritize what we consume. If we are to be people who continue to value truth, then cultivating discernment is nonnegotiable.

REALITY

As with truth, reality is not changing. What is changing is people's perception of reality. With the growing nuance and sophistication of media, virtual reality, and similar technologies, it is increasingly difficult to discern what is real from what is imaginary. Many of the comments I made about truth apply here. And as we have examined so far in this book, discerning the real from the unreal is of critical importance. Otherwise, we can find ourselves chasing after that which never existed, like the person striving for the physical features of a super model in a carefully edited photo.

RELIGION

Emerging technology is influencing almost every religion in some way. Where do people go when they have a faith question? While many still turn to their pastors or a learned family member or friend, countless others are literally googling God. They are typing questions into the most available search engine and exploring what appears at the top of the list. The question is, of course, what will they find there? Will the information lead them in the right direction or down a path to falsehood?

Searching for answers about theology and doctrine is certainly one way the digital culture is changing people's experience, but there are more examples. The web is far from neutral on matters of faith; messages with ethical implications and religious truth claims are all over the Internet. They are in the media and music we consume and the articles we read, and they're rampant on social media outlets.

By its very nature, the Internet is accessible to people of all faiths and provides ways for people to connect with one another. There are virtual church services. There are online discussion boards and "meeting places" that represent almost any contemporary religion. There are large bodies of content that represent different religions. And there are ample individual commentaries.

Such a way of experiencing religious messages is qualitatively different from what we have seen or experienced in the past. Yes, we have had libraries and diverse religious materials for almost as long as there has been written language. But as we've noted, our present time is the first time in history when so many different and competing sources are so readily available to almost anyone at any time. Interaction with these materials is often experienced apart from the guidance of a family member or spiritual leader— someone who can help us navigate it. Therefore, the ability to develop discernment with religious messages has never been more important than it is today. It is for this reason that, in the second half of this book, we will look at ways we can learn to navigate such a world.

One person explained online expressions of religion and spirituality to me this way: When you are in your own home, you can control the flow of content and messages quite easily. Historically, there was television and radio, which were simple to manage—tune in or turn off. Now we live in a world where it is common for a single household to have a half dozen devices, each one a gateway to an entire world of content. Many of us would not let our young kids wander the streets of New York City unsupervised, but many of us are doing the equivalent with access to the Internet, and many are quite comfortable with this. Of course, there are seldom immediate physical risks like those posed by walking the streets alone, but there are implications. The online world is a broad and diverse one with unfiltered messages and ideas that have an impact upon anyone who reads or consumes them. Yet easy access to unlimited information is so integrated in our lives that many of us have not taken the time to think strategically about how to manage the information flow. We welcome it into our homes and lives as if we were welcoming all of New York City into our living room.

The Sinful Nature

The ability to create and re-create the world around us challenges the very notion of what it means to be human. People now question ideas of what it means to be a human that were largely unchallenged in the past. God created us as social beings, but our digital world challenges basic notions of being social—what it means to communicate and interact with others, what it means to love and be loved, where to find the source of our worth and value, our greatest needs, and the solution to our greatest problems.

How does a world where so many things are customized and personalized to the individual change the way we think about ourselves and what it means to be human? How does it influence our expectations of others? How does it shape the way we understand and respond to messages about our sinfulness and need of a Savior? While humanity has grappled with these questions long before the current time, it seems evident that the digital world amplifies them, blurring our understanding of sin and leading us to new moral dilemmas and challenging our biblical view of humanity.

DISCUSSION AND REFLECTION QUESTIONS

- This chapter includes a list of potential changes partly brought about by emerging technology. Which of these changes are most prevalent in your life?

- Which of these changes are most prevalent in your family and church?

- Which of these changes are most prevalent in your school, workplace, or community?

- What other important changes have been brought about by the digital world?

PART 1: CONCLUSION

For Such a Time as This

While I offer reflections and questions, my purpose so far is to provide a cursory tour of some of the dominant elements of digital culture and its impact on Christians. My hope is that I have provided you with a starting point for your study and reflection, not a destination. We do not have quick and easy answers for these complex and ever-changing cultural issues.

We turn to the Scriptures as our source of truth. We gather with other believers and address questions about how we will respond. A pastor once confided to me that he sometimes wished we could return to simpler times, that these changes seemed overwhelming. He is not alone in that sentiment. Many of God's people in the Bible were not especially fond of the situations in which they found themselves. That may well have been how Esther felt when her cousin Mordecai said to her, "For if you keep silent at this time, relief and deliverance will rise for the Jews from another place, but you and your father's house will perish. And who knows whether you have not come to the kingdom for such a time as this" (Esther 4:14). God has placed us in our time, place, and culture to do His work through us too.

It is comforting to remember that we are not called to solve each one of the problems we have talked about in part 1. The problem of sin can never be resolved by man-made efforts or endeavors. We rest at the foot of the cross, trusting in God's mercy and following the Holy Spirit's guidance. From that context, we venture into the second half of this book to examine some of the possible responses to these concepts.

PART 2

HOW DO WE RESPOND?

In the first part of this book, we looked at a variety of ways technology can shape our thoughts, actions, families, communities, employment, and more. It is my hope that, by this time, it is clear that technology is not neutral and is indeed influencing each of us in many ways. It amplifies some values and beliefs while muzzling others. These influences occur over time and often in subtle ways, and they go beyond technology to become cultural and ideological.

After examining these particular trends, we will now consider how to respond to them. As Christians in the digital age, how will we live and react in a time such as this? How do we navigate faith and life in such a world? How do we help our families, our churches, and others make sense of all of this? These are the questions we will focus on in the second half of this book.

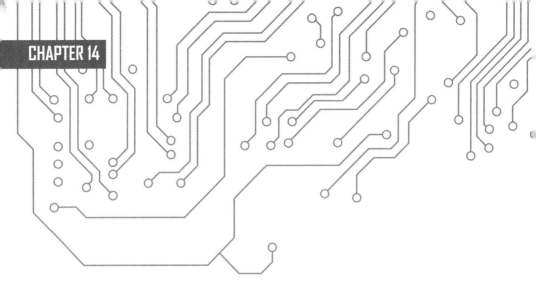

CHAPTER 14

What Has Not Changed?

After considering what seems like a constantly changing and fluid world, it is time to rest in what does not change. We can spend our entire lives chasing after understanding of the digital world only to find that it changes faster than we can grasp it. Or just as we have it in our hands (or minds), it disintegrates and disappears. New technologies overtake old ones. New forms of temptation emerge as others fade away. The world is in constant flux. But praise be to God that not everything is that way. Before we look at specific ways to respond to this digital world, this chapter encourages us to pause and ground ourselves in the things that do not change.

The Triune God

In Malachi, God reminds us, "For I the LORD do not change; therefore you, O children of Jacob, are not consumed" (3:6). In Hebrews, we read that "Jesus Christ is the same yesterday and today and forever" (13:8). While people might change their profile images constantly and while technologies come and go, we have a God who is beyond such fluidity and change, a God who is steady and consistent. He is not going anywhere.

God's Word

"The grass withers, the flower fades, but the word of our God will stand forever" (Isaiah 40:8). God's Word does not change. We can turn to it throughout all the seasons of our lives, and its relevance does not fade with the latest trend or technology. "For the word of God is living and active, sharper than any two-edged sword, piercing to the division of soul and of spirit, of joints and of marrow, and discerning the thoughts and intentions of the heart" (Hebrews 4:12). Such passages are anchors amid the shifting seas of our times. As we read in Matthew, "Everyone then who hears these words of Mine and does them will be like a wise man who built his house on the rock" (7:24). We will return to this throughout the second half of this book, given that any exploration of or engagement with the digital world is best done with our Bibles open.

In chapter 16, we will focus on the persistent relevance of God's Word. It can be easy for some people to dismiss the Bible as no longer relevant to these new and digital contexts, but nothing could be further from the truth! God's Word is as relevant as ever, though we do not always pause to consider how it applies to our times and circumstances. For example, just because the Bible does not mention social media, the Internet, or the latest technology by name does not mean God is silent on these issues.

HUMAN NATURE

Sin is a universal condition. "Surely there is not a righteous man on earth who does good and never sins" (Ecclesiastes 7:20). We know that "all have sinned and fall short of the glory of God" (Romans 3:23). Left to our own devices, we would use all of this technology to hoard for ourselves and seek complete independence from God, striving to set ourselves up as gods. In fact, that is precisely what we see when people claim that technology and science offer the solutions our superstitious ancestors sought from the omnipotent, omniscient, omnipresent, benevolent divine being. We can find countless quotes that claim as much.

What is important to recognize, however, is that science and technology, while offering many good things, are not solutions to our greatest and fundamental problem. They do not—and cannot—remedy our sinful condition. We find our ultimate solution only at the foot of the cross. God's love in Jesus Christ remains at the core as the solution to our greatest needs—forgiveness, salvation, reconciliation with our heavenly Father, hope, to name a few. As we considered in chapter 12, "What is desired in a man is steadfast love, and a poor man is better than a liar" (Proverbs 19:22). We cannot satisfy that desire by any technology or new scientific advancement.

FUNDAMENTAL HUMAN NEEDS AND DESIRES

Neuroscientists write about how technology is rewiring our brains, changing the way we think. Sociologists consider the implications of substituting digital connections to real-life human relationships and connections. Yet our most fundamental needs and desires are unchanging. We remain creations of God, designed to be in relationship with Him and with other people. We are relational beings by His design. In Ecclesiastes, we read, "He has put eternity into man's heart, yet so that he cannot find out what God has done from the beginning to the end" (3:11). We sense that there is something more, but we have no ability on our own to grasp it or comprehend it.

Furthermore, regardless of a person's age, locale, marital status, work, intellect, or technological savvy, we know that the individual has a fundamental human desire: relationship. We know this to be true of every person, even if we have never met him or her and know nothing else about him or her.

God's Promises

The Scriptures are full of promises from God, and every single one of them is reliable. We might not be able to discern truth from falsehood online. The digital world might be rampant with fake news, false promises, and inadequate solutions to our needs. But God always keeps His promises.

When I was twelve years old, my parents transferred me from the local public school to a nearby Lutheran school. The reason for the change was not for the Christian education as much as to remove me from a dangerous situation in the public school. On the way to school one day, another student put a knife to my throat and threatened to kill me at the end of the day. I spent much of the morning hiding and throwing up in the bathroom, afraid to tell anyone. Fortunately, a friend told the principal, and he intervened. Since there was still uncertainty about my safety, my parents moved me to another school. At Zion Lutheran School in Bethalto, Illinois, I found myself in a much safer and more positive learning environment. I quickly made new friends. I also arrived in time to participate in the day school confirmation classes. The pastor taught from God's Word and Martin Luther's Small Catechism. What he taught engaged and fascinated me. While some of this might have been familiar to the other students, I was new to the Christian school, so it was all fresh, new, and exciting to me. I remember getting overzealous at times, stretching my arm as high as possible to be called on to answer the next question.

I spent only one semester at that school before my father's work called for us to move to Texas, a situation that was also short-lived. Not long after we moved into our new home in Texas, my father, who had struggled with health issues, died of heart problems. I vividly remember sitting in the back room of our house as my mother made those difficult calls to family members, sharing the news of my father's death and arranging for us to move close to other relatives. Sitting in our back room, my semester of lessons about God's love for us in Jesus Christ was an anchor and incredible source of comfort and stability, even as everything around me seemed in flux. In those moments, the Psalms and other Bible passages took on special meaning for me. I clung to God's promises, which never change. "Even though I walk through the valley of the shadow of death, I will fear no evil, for You are with me; Your rod and Your staff, they comfort me" (Psalm 23:4).

Even as I, a twelve-year-old, grappled with the implication of being fatherless, I found comfort in the fact that I was not alone. "And behold, I am with you always, to the end of the age" (Matthew 28:20). As I write about this more than thirty years later, I still find myself holding back the tears. These are not tears of sadness as much as they are tears of joy and gratitude that we have a God who keeps His promises. We have a God who is with us always, a God whose love is so great that He was willing to sacrifice His own Son to save us from our sin and secure a place for us with Him for eternity. In the following chapters, as we consider how we might respond to faith and life in this digital age, I hope you, too, will let the fact that God and His Word are unchanging be a constant source of comfort and strength—now and always.

DISCUSSION AND REFLECTION QUESTIONS

- Of the list of unchanging aspects of life in this chapter, which ones give you the most comfort at this moment in your life?

- Beyond those mentioned in this chapter, what other aspects of life do not change? What keeps you grounded in this world of seemingly constant change?

- Reflecting on the ideas in this chapter, what do you think is most important for people to hear—whether in your home, church, school, community, workplace, or beyond? How might you share these insights with them in a caring and winsome way?

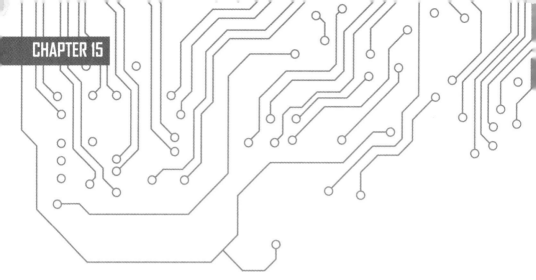

CHAPTER 15

Think like a Missionary

There is a longstanding and constant tension between Christ and culture, and there are few areas where this is more apparent than in the lives of missionaries whom God calls to be witnesses to the Gospel of Jesus Christ to entirely different cultures. Yet, when a missionary moves to a new place, serving is usually not as simple as starting to preach the Gospel. The missionary must take time to learn the language, learn the culture, and build relationships. This is an intense and time-consuming process, but it is an important part of the work.

We learn in Acts 17 that Paul observed what was going on in this powerful city at the heart of the Greek way of life and religion. When he was invited to speak in their pagan assembly, the Areopagus, he started in a fascinating way: by referencing the culture. He explained that he could see that the people were religious. They were so religious that they had an idol to an unknown god. Then, Paul used that concept already within Athenian culture to preach the Gospel. Paul explained that he was there in Athens to introduce them to a God who is indeed unknown to them. Paul continued by telling them about how Jesus' death and resurrection reveals the true God to us, the Lord of heaven and earth. Along the way, Paul even quoted Greek poetry. In other words, he drew from familiar items in their culture to teach them about Jesus.

This same opportunity exists for Christians today. As we study and learn about this modern digital culture, we find ways to share the Gospel with others. This calls for us to approach life with a missionary mind-set. We wander the digital streets. We listen. We learn. We prayerfully consider the implications of this digital world, doing so with

God's Word open and understanding that it speaks directly to the important issues in this context.

There is much we can glean from a missionary mind-set in the digital world. In my conversations with others who served as missionaries, as well as the example of the great missionaries in the Scriptures, I offer the following ten starting points as we think about what it means to embrace a missionary mind-set in an increasingly digital world. I summarize them here and will expand on them in the subsequent chapters.

1. REMAIN GROUNDED IN THE WORD

In Hebrews 4:12, we are reminded that "the word of God is living and active, sharper than any two-edged sword, piercing to the division of soul and of spirit, of joints and of marrow, and discerning the thoughts and intentions of the heart." A friend once told me how people are trained to identify counterfeit currency. Since it's nearly impossible to train people on all the possible ways that counterfeit money looks and feels, the training focuses on teaching people to recognize the real thing. So, if you know all the key features of authentic money, then, ideally, it is much easier to identify what is counterfeit.

Whether or not this is actually how people are trained to identify counterfeit currency, the concept is applicable to us here. If we are going to navigate this constantly changing digital world, then we are wise to start with what does not change: God's Word, the norm and source of doctrine for Christians. "Heaven and earth will pass away, but My words will never pass away" (Matthew 24:35). Then, with our Bibles open (literally), we begin to examine the challenges and opportunities of this current context. Of course, this is not a one-time occurrence, but something we do regularly. We read, study, and learn from the exposition of the Word as it is preached and taught in the Divine Service. As we do, the Holy Spirit is equipping us for the challenges of discerning good and evil, right and wrong, wisdom and foolishness.

2. KNOW YOUR AUDIENCE

As I advised earlier in this chapter, it is wise to think about the people, not just the technology involved in these topics. When I consider the challenges and opportunities in the digital world, I find it helpful to set aside my assumptions in order to listen to others' thoughts and learn from their experiences. I am not suggesting that we adopt their positions or agree with people who think differently from us but rather that we take the time to listen and learn. In doing so, we will come to better understand their beliefs, values, fears, joys, and challenges.

I once gave a talk to a group of grandparents who wanted to better connect with their grandchildren who seemed increasingly attached to their phones and screens. We met three times, and at the end of the first evening, I gave them all a homework assignment. I asked them to spend an hour or two with a grandchild over the next week, asking the grandchild to take them on a tour of their "digital lives." The job of the grandparents was to be deeply curious. Ask questions that interest their grandchildren. Do not just ask about how to do things on the device. Ask what they like and do not like. Ask why they use different apps, games, or programs. Try not to judge or preach. Just love, listen, learn, and be curious.

In the second session, we debriefed about how their homework went with the grandchildren. Many of the participants were anxious to tell their stories. They were amazed at how much the grandchildren opened up to them. Some reported that their grandchildren said they were the first to ask them about their activities. Some grandchildren shared fears and concerns. One confessed to a serious cyberbullying issue, allowing the grandparent to intervene. Others asked their grandparents questions, seeking their advice on different situations and thinking aloud about moral dilemmas.

I do not want to overstate what happened. It was not some sudden and magical transformation. However, it gave the grandparents a very real and personal understanding of their grandchildren's digital lives, and it created future opportunities for conversation. It offered them insight that is hard to get from a book or article.

In the world of public speaking and writing, for example, we say, "Know your audience." This is an important part of being a missionary, a teacher, or communicator. We can learn a great deal from reading about various issues, but we also learn from the ideas with skin. By that, I mean that I like to meet the people who cling to certain ideas, beliefs, and values. As I advised the grandparents, I try to first listen so I can learn. That way I develop a better understanding of the issue so I can determine how to respond when and if the opportunity arises.

3. BUILD RELATIONSHIPS

A benefit of the grandparent homework assignment was that the grandparents deepened their relationships with their grandchildren by spending quality time together. This is an important part of our grappling with some of the challenges and opportunities of life in a digital world. We are wise to build positive and trusting relationships. Within those relationships, we are then willing to be vulnerable and candid about our beliefs, values, doubts, fears, challenges, and questions. If we do not know about these things, then it is difficult to address them. Building trust and relationship is the important starting point.

4. Test Your Assumptions

If missionaries are going to be faithful to the Scriptures, then their work calls for separating personal preferences, cultural norms, and comfort zones from what the Scriptures teach. The missionary's job is not to be a champion for his or her home culture, but to make disciples. Yet, this is not always easy. Our frame of reference is the culture in which we grew up, and we come to see certain practices as the right way to do things. We may treat mere cultural preferences, traditions, and norms as if they were God-ordained matters of right and wrong. This can lead us into prideful thinking and away from a position of humility.

If we examine changing technology throughout history, we can find many examples of people who thought that the adoption of a new technology was dangerous and needed to be resisted. Some people thought that about the written word. People worried about that with the printing press—that their children would read too much. If we scoured the archives, we would find similar criticisms about telephones, radio, television, and most certainly the Internet. In general, people can be cautious about and sometimes critical of the unknown. At the same time, some of these critics might have been right about their concerns. Perhaps the written word did decrease our ability to memorize long narratives, or at least it decreased our value for that skill. Perhaps the written word did lead to some children becoming less active—a concern many have voiced about the television. This continues to remind us of a recurring point in this book, that all technologies bring with them both affordances and limitations.

Yet, there is still a measure of humility we can learn from this. There will be times when the impact of some technology is clearly counter to God's Word, and we are compelled to speak out about it. At the same time, it is wise if we are not too quick to jump to such a conclusion as we think about the changes in our digital world. This is part of why I advise that we first think in terms of affordances and limitations instead of quickly labeling something as right or wrong. Television has clearly filled our minds with explicit images, but it has also served as a powerful tool for education, as a way to share the Good News of Jesus Christ, and as a means to create and tell positive and influential stories. A social media platform like Facebook has amplified bullying and sometimes seems to bring out the worst in us as we interact with one another, but it is also a powerful way for families and friends to stay connected. This is true for many, perhaps even most, technologies. There are benefits and there are limitations.

5. The Role of Words and Actions

Missionaries know that the people around them are watching. What they say and do may open—or close—doors to future conversations, relationships, and ministry. While Christian freedom leaves room for certain words and actions, we are wise to heed Paul's admonition: "But take care that this right of yours does not somehow become a stumbling block to the weak" (1 Corinthians 8:9). There may be nothing morally wrong or explicitly forbidden in Scripture about some of the decisions we make on social media or in the larger digital world, but there is a persistent reminder that those around us observe our words and actions. Those of us in the vocation of parent, friend, teacher, pastor, and citizen, for example, heed this wisdom as we make decisions in this contemporary age.

6. Be Genuine

Sometimes we want to be seen as someone who has it all together. We are tempted to act as if we have everything figured out, so we worry that a lack of knowledge or confidence might reflect poorly on us. There is always wisdom in prayerfully considering what we share and how we share it, both in interpersonal interactions and via social media. It can also be valuable for others to see that we do not have everything figured out. Learning to navigate faith and life in this digital world can be challenging and confusing. We will make mistakes. We will give in to the temptations of sin. Instead of hiding or denying our flaws and failures, we begin by confessing our sins to God. We pray for strength to overcome our fears, uncertainties, and inadequacies. And when appropriate, we can share some of these struggles with others, allowing them to provide encouragement and admonishment as fellow brothers and sisters in Christ, but also so that the struggles of others are not exacerbated by the false idea that everyone else has it figured out. We can join in learning together, holding one another accountable, and providing support and encouragement when needed.

7. Patience and Prayer for Opportunities

In James 1:19, we are reminded, "Know this, my beloved brothers: let every person be quick to hear, slow to speak, slow to anger." In an age of instant everything, we may need a reminder that listening and learning take patience. Some of the grandparents in the story related earlier may have been tempted to interrupt their grandchild and lecture about why something is wrong or foolish. While there is a time for such discussions, deepening relationships with others takes time. For missionaries, there is a persistent tension between the urgency of sharing an important message from God's

Word and waiting for a good opportunity for such a candid conversation. A large part of what I am arguing for in this book is that we create space in our churches and homes where we can talk more openly about the influence of digital culture upon our faith and lives, thereby also creating opportunities to join together in learning how God's Word applies to these new and changing contexts.

8. Participation but Not Compromise

One of the ways we learn about the digital culture is through what some researchers call participant observation. This occurs when we both engage in the activities ourselves and at the same time observe—taking note of what we see and experience, and taking time to analyze and learn from the experience. The author of Romans puts it this way, "Do not be conformed to this world, but be transformed by the renewal of your mind, that by testing you may discern what is the will of God, what is good and acceptable and perfect" (12:2).

I am not suggesting that every one of us should try every app, join every social media site, and buy and use every new tech gadget. Some of us may be called to the ongoing work of carefully analyzing such things, leading to greater involvement, but that is unlikely the call of every Christian. However, there is much to be learned by carefully and deliberately experiencing aspects of this digital world. Almost all of us do this already. Only now, the challenge is to do it more intentionally and consider the implications of our experiences. At the same time, we are also cautious of justifying sinful thoughts and behavior under the guise of "research." One need not become a drug user or alcoholic to be a witness to others who use drugs and drink. The same principle applies when we think about various activities in the digital world.

9. Confession and Absolution

As I mentioned in the section about being genuine, no good comes from denying or ignoring sinful thoughts, words, and actions. When we recognize our sin (or when another helps us to see our sin), we heed the wisdom found in 1 John: "If we say we have no sin, we deceive ourselves, and the truth is not in us. If we confess our sins, He is faithful and just to forgive us our sins and to cleanse us from all unrighteousness" (1:8–9). As we participate in Confession and Absolution in the Divine Service, God brings His gift of forgiveness, which is also an important part of being equipped to face the challenges and embrace the opportunities in this digital age.

10. Collaboration and Fellowship

Considering faith and life in our digital age need not be a Lone Ranger endeavor.

As you will find in the upcoming chapters, there are many ways we can come together as a family, as friends, as co-workers, and as members of a congregation or small group to think, pray, study, and consider our faith and life in the digital world. We need not think we are all alone in the challenges of faith the come with life in the digital world. There is the temptation for some people, for example, to believe that online communities are places where they can be more open and candid, where they can be their true selves. While I do not deny the usefulness of such communities for some people, it is important for us to create trusting and caring environments in our homes and churches for such relationship building.

LOOKING AHEAD

This list of ten ways to embrace a missionary mind-set in an increasingly digital world is not an exhaustive list, but in my experience, it is a helpful starting point as we come up with a more intentional plan to live out our faith in these new contexts. Now, with some of these basic ideas set at the foundation, each of the following chapters offers suggestions or ideas on how we might promote greater thought, prayer, and study about digital culture and our lives in it.

DISCUSSION AND REFLECTION QUESTIONS

- Which of the missionary traits listed in this chapter require the most attention for you at this point in your life?

- How do you try to get to know the digital culture and world today without compromising your beliefs and values?

- Near the end of this chapter, we looked at the role of collaboration and fellowship when it comes to exploring faith and life in the digital world. With whom do you collaborate and discuss these matters? Or if you currently do not collaborate or discuss with others, with whom would you like to start collaborating and discussing these matters?

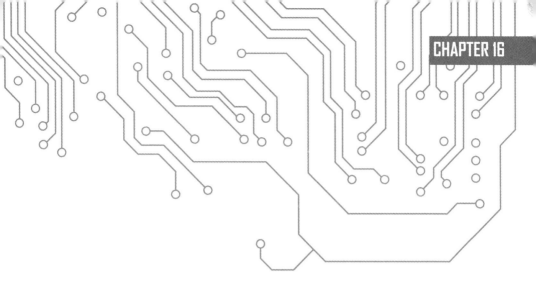

CHAPTER 16

God's Word as a Lamp and Guide in the Digital World

The psalmist prays, "Your word is a lamp to my feet and a light to my path" (Psalm 119:105). As we have discussed, the significance and relevance of God's Word does not fade with changing fads, innovations, technologies, and shifting cultures. That is an incredible comfort for us as Christians. When Peter made the great confession that Jesus is the Christ, the Son of the living God, Jesus replied, "And I tell you, you are Peter, and on this rock I will build My church, and the gates of hell shall not prevail against it" (Matthew 16:18). That confession of Peter is an unchanging rock for us individually as Christians and collectively as the Church. Jesus tells us that "heaven and earth will pass away, but My words will not pass away" (Luke 21:33). Without something consistent and stable and true, we can quickly find ourselves lost and chasing after every new idea or trend, trusting it as a savior from our greatest fears, challenges, and problems. God's Word, however, grounds us in all situations.

At the same time, some of us fall prey to compartmentalizing what we learn from God's Word. Teachers, in particular, see this happening. It can be described as a problem in the transfer of learning: We learn something in one context but find it difficult to transfer the concept to a different situation or setting. We might not even think that what we learned applies to other situations. For instance, a parent teaches table manners to a child at home, but when they go out to dinner at a restaurant, the child does not seem to remember or care about manners. The parents wonder what went wrong. We often tie a lesson to the situation in which we learned it. It usually takes some work and intentionality to help ourselves and others see that these lessons apply to other situations as well.

I have seen this same behavior in my study of people and their online actions. To illustrate the point, let us go through five of the Ten Commandments, reflecting on how they apply to the digital world.

"You shall have no other gods before Me" (Exodus 20:3).

As discussed in chapter 12, technology can become an idol, something we lean on and trust above God. If someone were to place a giant, golden idol of a false god in front of us and tell us to bow down and worship it, we would readily recognize the sin and refuse. Another example is comparing the teachings of the Christian faith to those of other religions. You get the idea. Yet ubiquitous technologies and devices hold the potential of becoming our idols. Because our preoccupation occurs gradually, we may not recognize it as idolatry.

"Honor your father and your mother, that your days may be long in the land the LORD your God is giving you" (Exodus 20:12).

Maybe we get the idea that mocking our parents is not a good idea, that it breaks the Fourth Commandment. And we recognize that the same goes for not respecting those who are placed in positions of authority over us. Yet something comes over some of us when we are online or sending an email or a text. We say things about those in authority that tears them down and disrespects them. We repost something that ridicules a politician, or we forward an article that critiques or condemns from a one-sided perspective. The Small Catechism teaches that "we should fear and love God so that we do not despise or anger our parents and other authorities, but honor them, serve and obey them, love and cherish them" (explanation of the Fourth Commandment). The Small Catechism explains that "other authorities" include "all those whom God has placed over us at home, in government, at school, at the place where we work, and in the church." It goes on to say, "God forbids us to despise our parents and other authorities by not respecting them or angering them by our disobedience or by any other kind of sin" (Christian Questions, 48–49).

"You shall not murder" (Exodus 20:13).

Harming others with our words is one way we break the Fifth Commandment, and social media has changed the nature of our interaction with others. When we respond in harsh ways to or about people online, we do so from a distance. We are separated by our computer monitors or device. This distance can cause us to think of our comments or the recipients of our comments as less real. This common online behavior is sometimes called *disembodied communication*. We fall into the trap of thinking of our comments as "just words." When we say something hurtful, we do not see the other person's nonverbals—his or her sadness, hurt, disappointment, or tears. We cannot control how the person on the receiving end interprets what we post. And for our part, we may not experience the same rush of emotions at the seriousness of our words. Our actions seem a little less real and less serious than they would if we were face-to-face with the other person.

This is a serious problem in social media outlets and electronic communication, even email. A company once hired me to spend a day teaching their employees about email etiquette. They found that many people in the company seemed rude or even mean in their emails, and it was hurting the culture in the organization. As part of my presentation, I prepared a few fictional emails that resembled the types of emails that were the impetus for my visit. I asked for two volunteers to come up to the front of the room and sit in chairs facing one another. I handed a printed-out email conversation to each of them, asking them to take turns reading it while trying to make direct eye contact with the other person.

The activity was painful to watch and even more painful for the volunteers. People in the audience gasped at times, and more than a few people began to stare at the floor, unable to make eye contact with others. This set the stage for talking about the words that we use via email and how they can affect other people. In fact, nothing I taught that day was new. Much of what I shared were lessons I learned in my childhood home, school, church, and Sunday School. Nonetheless, the digital distance of email had become a barrier for some people to transfer basic but important lessons about how we treat one another.

Many of us witnessed this on social media in 2016, an especially contentious election year. The intensity of comments, anger, and harsh statements reached an all-time high. It became so strong that I found myself in a near constant state of anger and frustration over what I was seeing and reading. I even found myself tempted to join in the banter. Jesus taught, "If your right eye causes you to sin, tear it out and throw it away. For it is better that you lose one of your members than that your whole body be thrown into hell" (Matthew 5:29). Heeding the wisdom of that passage, I decided to log off the social media outlet until the election was over and things returned closer to normal.

Yet "normal" online is not usually the same as "normal" in the face-to-face world. Many of us, emboldened or numbed by the physical separation from the person to whom or about whom we are writing, are tempted to write things we would probably not say to that person's face. We ridicule celebrities and politicians. We share harsh criticisms of photos. We express things that we would not express in the physical world. Isolated in a digital bubble, we do not necessarily think of the harsh words we share as Fifth Commandment issue, but they are.

"You shall not commit adultery" (Exodus 20:14).

To make a point, I am going to tell you a fictional story. I need to emphasize that this is fictional. Back in the 1990s, chat rooms were quite popular online. You could go to a web page, see a list of topics, click on one, and find yourself in a virtual room with a few or a lot of other people who were all interested in "talking" about a certain topic. But this was a text-based conversation. You could type a message, and a stream of other typed messages flowed from the bottom of your screen to the top. You could also send a private message just between you and another person, a message that was visible only to the two of you.

In this fictitious example, I was in one of those rooms, and another person who went by the name "Princess" started sending private messages to me. The messages grew increasingly flirtatious, even asking me about what I was doing that night. I am a married man, so it would be especially inappropriate to entertain such propositions, but imagine that I did. I reply to the person, flirting back with her. Now imagine that my wife walks into the room, smiles at me, and asks if I like her new screen name—"Princess." Imagine that it was my wife flirting with me in that chat room. She was just flirting with her husband, and I was just flirting with my wife. But in the moment, my motives were far less pure than what was going on in reality.

This fictional situation highlights the importance of motives and illustrates one of many Sixth Commandment temptations exacerbated by the digital age. This scenario is among the less likely ones, but the amount of pornography, sexually explicit media, and websites intentionally designed to help people cheat on their spouses, share and view explicit images, and arrange casual sexual encounters with strangers is staggering.

Temptations of this type have been around long before the invention of the Internet, of course, but its power and features amplify them. Add to this the ideas I shared in the section about the Fifth Commandment. The Internet not only magnifies the temptation to treat people differently than we would in person but also tempts us to see online communication as less real (or at least not as serious) as face-to-face conversations. Therefore, we have a perfect storm of temptation.

"You shall not steal" (Exodus 20:15).

If there were a CD in a store that we wanted, we probably would not have a strong temptation to take it without paying for it. Yet taking recordings without paying for them was a commonplace activity around 2000 when Napster made it easy for people to download music, freely but also illegally. The law eventually caught up with Napster and shut down the operation, but this speaks to the temptations online. Either we don't understand the idea of property, or the reality of property might not seem as real when we are online. People who would never think of stealing property in the physical world are tempted when the item is in digital form. We copy and paste images online without permission. We use the words or ideas of others without giving them credit or seeking permission. When everything is so readily available and so easily captured, shared, or reused, we might not recognize that these, too, are Seventh Commandment issues. The creators of images, music, and online content are neighbors whom we are called to love, and part of loving them includes respecting their rights and property.

WHAT DOES THIS MEAN?

These examples further illustrate the problem of transfer. Many of us know biblical teachings and understand how they apply to common situations in our daily lives, but we are challenged to apply the same teachings to the digital world or when a new technology makes certain things possible that were not before.

This problem is not limited to social media. The larger digital and technological world includes countless medical technologies that sometimes clash with our core convictions as Christians, especially when it comes to the protection of human life. Some technologies may clash with one or more of the Ten Commandments, but because these technologies are new and the situation is unfamiliar, we do not necessarily think to ask how God's Word can inform our thoughts and actions. For example, one mobile phone app is called Gossip. The creators advertise it as an app to help you anonymously gossip. While people could use it for other purposes, this app could also be a temptation to participate in digitized gossip.

However, even when we do ask tough questions, the answers are not always clear. Consider the app Snapchat, which allows you to send messages to others that disappear or delete themselves after a set period of time. Many saw this as an app that encourages and frees people to share inappropriate images without them being saved permanently. Yet, it developed into a more widely used app that plenty of people use responsibly to communicate with friends or even family members. There may be times when even after careful study, ambiguous situations remain. Therefore, it is all the more important that we not simply create a list of what to do and not to do, memorize it, and try to follow it. This is something we would be wise to address with ongoing conversations, prayer, and reflection. Even in this information age, many people are not sure where to go for wisdom and guidance on what to do. Conversely, they want a quick and definitive answer when the question is not always that simple.

If a simple list of dos and don'ts is not sufficient, if the answers to these questions are unclear even after a good measure of study, if we don't even know where to begin to look for guidance, then what are we to do? In my work with students, parents, grandparents, and educators, I find a simple approach works best when facilitating healthy conversation. I find four key elements to be effective.

1. You need a group of interested and willing people who can commit to a regular gathering time. This group can be composed of family members, a few friends, a small group at church, or co-workers who meet over lunch.

2. Every participant has a Bible, preferably a study Bible.

3. Each person in the group comes prepared to discuss questions and concerns about life in this digital age.

4. A wise facilitator guides the conversation. In many situations, this role is filled by a pastor, but it might also be a parent, a Bible study leader, or someone else who agrees to facilitate.

Once these four elements are in place, it is necessary to set an agenda. The group agrees on a question or challenge to explore. Prior to the meeting, participants scour the Scriptures to seek wisdom and insight on the challenge or question. Then they gather to pray, share their findings, and discuss them. What naturally occurs is a robust conversation where members of the group expand on the topic. They ask related questions. They share life experiences. They encourage and challenge one another. Most important, they turn to God in prayer and seek out wisdom from His Word.

In the times when I have had the privilege to facilitate these gatherings, they have been personally rewarding, and others in the group report as much. Notice that this gathering is not the result of some grand or elaborate planning. It is simply a gathering that creates the conditions in which people are able to take the time to explore the relevance of God's Word for the new and distinct situations created by the digital world.

There are common challenges that arise in such groups, however, so it is helpful to keep in mind the following five tips to keep the conversation fruitful and edifying and to avoid falling into some theological traps.

Remember: Scripture Trumps Experience

Many of us love to tell stories about our experiences, and those stories play an important role in the way we think about how God's Word applies to different situations. Our experiences help us relate to what we are studying. Stories keep the conversation practical, and they help us get to know and relate to one another. The problem arises when our stories serve as the guide for truth claims. God's Word is the source of truth. Our experiences can give us context and insights, but it is important to remember a passage mentioned earlier: "All Scripture is breathed out by God and profitable for teaching, for reproof, for correction, and for training in righteousness, that the man of God may be complete, equipped for every good work" (2 Timothy 3:16–17). We draw on our experiences as we seek wisdom to inform our thoughts and actions; we do not conform Scripture to our experiences.

Keep in Mind Law and Gospel

Because groups will discuss moral challenges, there is a persistent temptation to want clear directions listing what to do and what not to do. This is not always possible, so I caution readers to beware of falling into the trap of legalism, believing that a list of laws will make everything better. If we resist this temptation, small-group gatherings can be a place where we recognize our sinful thoughts and actions, repent, remember our forgiveness in Jesus Christ, and consider how to respond moving forward. This is a beautiful thing to witness and experience.

Be Patient in Your Search for Answers

I have mentioned this many times because I often find people struggling with the stress of having unanswered questions. Sometimes we just want clear-cut answers. Is this a good technology or a bad one? What is the most responsible use of this technology? Yet, as we have discovered throughout this book, there are many nuances to most situations. I encourage people to be patient but continue in their search for answers. Jumping to conclusions or moving on too quickly can lead to missing important faith lessons. We call these moral dilemmas for a reason. We want to discern what is good and right, but we do not want to go to the other extreme and assume that anything goes, that all technologies are good and right.

BUILD TRUST

Building trust in groups takes time. Doubts, fears, and struggles are not the sort of things that most of us are comfortable sharing in front of others. Some people are more reserved than others. But the goal of this group is not to get everyone sharing his or her deepest and darkest secrets. The goal is to build a community where people feel safe enough to share their thoughts and questions. This environment usually benefits from having a few ground rules for the group. It is a useful exercise for the group to establish their own ground rules, adding some shared ownership. However, I argue that there are a few nonnegotiables when it comes to the role of God's Word.

PRIORITIZE LEARNING OVER DEBATING

Sometimes debates are rich, respectful, and conducive to learning, but the purpose of this group is not to debate every topic. Your group gathers to explore the relevance of God's Word upon modern life, thought, trends, and events. It is important for everyone in the group to agree with this goal and to join in redirecting one another when and if the debate becomes more central than the shared goal of learning together.

THE CENTRAL POINT

I suggest a group like this as one of the ways to approach the study of God's Word as it relates to the digital age. There are, of course, many other ways this happens. It might happen as an integrated part of existing Bible studies and Sunday School. It could be part of a book talk. It might happen a little more informally over conversations at the family dinner table or on road trips. It might also come amid one's personal devotional time and Bible readings. All of these opportunities align with the instruction of how to use the Ten Commandments as recorded in the Book of Deuteronomy:

> Now this is the commandment—the statutes and the rules—that the LORD your God commanded me to teach you, that you may do them in the land to which you are going over, to possess it, that you may fear the LORD your God, you and your son and your son's son, by keeping all His statutes and His commandments, which I command you, all the days of your life, and that your days may be long. Hear therefore, O Israel, and be careful to do them, that it may go well with you, and that you may multiply greatly, as the LORD, the God of your fathers, has promised you, in a land flowing with milk and honey. Hear, O Israel: The LORD our God, the LORD is one. You shall love the LORD your God with all your heart and

with all your soul and with all your might. And these words that I command you today shall be on your heart. You shall teach them diligently to your children, and shall talk of them when you sit in your house, and when you walk by the way, and when you lie down, and when you rise. You shall bind them as a sign on your hand, and they shall be as frontlets between your eyes. You shall write them on the doorposts of your house and on your gates. (6:1–9)

Notice the relevance of this passage to what we are exploring together, but also recognize how it happens. It does not just happen in those formal groups or study times. This is something about which we can talk throughout the day. We do so as we travel from one place to another. We "teach them diligently" to our children (v. 7). We talk about them at home and ponder them as we go to bed at night. We establish reminders for ourselves of these teachings. There is nothing new for us here. It is just that we find ourselves in different contexts that call for us to learn anew how these truths apply to our lives.

DISCUSSION AND REFLECTION QUESTIONS

- In this chapter, we considered the danger of compartmentalizing biblical teachings—applying them in one part of life, but not everywhere. Describe instances of this compartmentalizing that you notice in your life, family, church, community, school, or workplace.

- As you read the list of Commandments and their applications to the digital world, what is one area that you think calls for special attention from you or those around you?

- What can you do to promote greater reflection and discussion about the application of God's Word to current and emerging digital contexts?

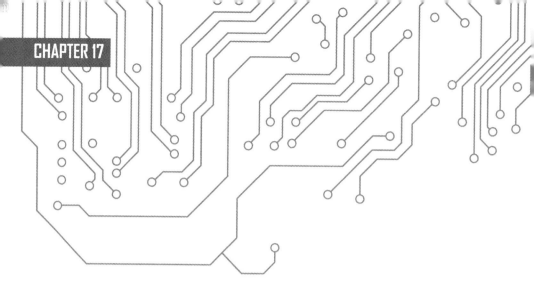

CHAPTER 17

Bible-Based Media Literacy and Digital Discernment

Making sense of this digital landscape requires a specific set of tools and skills, as I alluded to in chapter 5. Managing the inundation of messages in this digital world calls for the cultivation of a new type of literacy, one that is Bible-based. Before I explain what I mean by that, I will begin with a couple of stories.

THE PRESIDENTIAL CANDIDATE

Many years ago, I attended a campaign event for someone who was running for President of the United States. The candidate was scheduled to arrive on a train, and those in attendance were carefully positioned alongside the track where he intended to stop. When I arrived at the event, there were security guards and campaign workers who sorted us. They directed anyone with an oppositional sign into a small area in the back corner, away from where the video cameras for the major television stations were set up. Any horns and megaphones were confiscated. Those who were identified as supporters were directed to the front and center. I do not think anyone forced us to put away the homemade signs we had brought with us, but they firmly asked us to set them down. We were handed one of the carefully designed signs intended to communicate the three main points the candidate intended to talk about on that day.

As we took our new signs and gathered into our assigned positions, a train arrived, but it was not the one the candidate was on. This was a person assigned with the task of preparing us for the candidate's arrival. He came out of the back of the train and taught us a few chants and cheers, essentially giving us a short lesson on what to say and when to hold up different signs.

Then the candidate arrived, talked with us for twenty to thirty minutes, and left. We followed the instructions with our signs and chanted just as we had rehearsed. The opposition was unheard and unseen. They were far enough in the back that even if someone shouted protests, those of us in the front would not have heard it.

That evening, I turned on the evening news and saw a clip about the event I had attended only a few hours before. As I watched, it felt as if I were watching an entirely different event. What I saw on television seemed so natural, unrehearsed, authentic, and festive—far from the rehearsed event I experienced hours before. Nonetheless, the positive event the candidate and the team wanted to convey was exactly what appeared that evening on the news.

The Olympians

On the night of February 16, 2014, the men's super G for the Winter Olympics was televised, and two Americans medaled in silver and bronze. Christin Cooper, a fifty-four-year-old former alpine skier who worked as a broadcaster for NBC, interviewed the medalists. She asked silver medalist Andrew Weibrecht a couple of questions, but then devoted the rest of her time to interviewing Bode Miller. Her line of questioning was, from early on, insensitive toward Miller, asking about the death of his brother in the past year, whether or not he was emotional, and what he was thinking when he looked up at the sky before starting his races. A tactful journalist would have stopped after a couple of questions. However, she kept going. And her last question was, I thought, over-the-top, insensitive, and even bullying.[52] At minimum, it seemed like an obvious attempt to conjure tears from the vulnerable Miller.

I remember feeling frustrated and embarrassed that NBC aired such a broadcast and angry at what seemed to be tactless and hurtful questioning. My frustration grew when I went to the NBC Olympics website a few minutes later. On the main page was a large image and video of Bode Miller with the subtitle "Bode's higher purpose: A year after his brother's death, Bode Miller's emotions finally caught up after winning bronze in super G."[53] Anyone watching that interview knew the description was, at minimum, deceptive. It was far from an accurate representation of the events. In my opinion, "Bode Miller badgered by insensitive questions after earning bronze medal" would have been the more accurate headline.

As I watched the interview, I saw no evidence that Miller was interested in continuing the conversation. Fortunately, we do not need to depend upon a single news source

---

52   "Does NBC's Christin Cooper Push Bode Miller Too Far?" YouTube, February 17, 2014 https://www.youtube.com/watch?v=ClsrmAXSEDU (accessed March 19, 2017).

53   This article has since been removed from the Internet.

to get more of the story. We can read other reports, such as "NBC reporter badgers Bode Miller about dead brother till he cries"[54]; "NBC's Christin Cooper True Snow Snob with USA's Bode Miller"[55]; and similar blog posts and articles. A quick review of such sources can reinforce the value of multiple media sources for news coverage.

These examples serve as helpful reminders about how truth can be represented in contemporary media. They illustrate the fact that some reporting on local, national, and even world events is rarely neutral and sometimes even inaccurate. It is limiting to trust a single broadcasting outlet as one's go-to news source. This emphasizes the importance of cultivating information literacy and media literacy skills necessary to digest multiple perspectives and discern the truth. In today's world, a critical eye for news media is more necessary than ever.

The campaign event and the Olympics news broadcast were both eye-opening experiences for me, causing me to realize the careful construction of most everything I experience on the screen, whether television, computer, or smartphone. Even many of the "informal" YouTube videos we see today are set and crafted to some extent. What I "read" when I watch a video online is quite often edited and constructed with intent. Of course, we could say the same thing about any book, including this one. I use some words and not others, some examples and not others. Yet, there is a difference between a book and visual media. If you cannot read a book, it cannot directly influence you very much. If you are unable to read, an image or video can still influence you.

How much more important is this fact given that the majority of moral claims and religious messages we experience today come via the many media sources embedded in our daily lives? Some people learn about Christianity only from YouTube videos, films and sitcoms, online articles, news reports, and posts on social media. The originators of this media construct it with intentionality. In many cases, their goal is not to simply give the facts but to influence how and what we think about them. Experts influence public opinion through intentional representation of any number of topics and social issues. Media outlets have the power to set the agenda for public discourse and to influence how we think about what they share with us.[56]

How much time do you spend consuming media each day? One source from 2016

---

54   Mike Dyce, "NBC reporter badgers Bode Miller about dead brother till he cries (Video)," FanSided, February 16, 2014, http://fansided.com/2014/02/16/nbc-reporter-badgers-bode-miller-dead-brother-till-cries/ (accessed March 19, 2017).

55   Steve Huisel, "NBC's Christin Cooper True Snow Snob with USA's Bode Miller," *ChicagoNow*, February 16, 2014, http://www.chicagonow.com/chicago-sports-fan-talk/2014/02/nbcs-christin-cooper-true-snow-snob-with-usas-bode-miller/ (accessed March 19, 2017).

56   Maxwell McCombs, *Setting the Agenda: The Mass Media and Public Opinion* (Hoboken, NJ: Wiley, 2013), ix.

points to adults consuming more than ten hours of media a day, much of that from television, computers, mobile phones, and other mobile devices.[57] The amount of time many of us spend consuming a steady diet of media and the extent to which that media sets the agenda is too important of a topic for us to ignore, especially in regard to our families, schools, and churches. Marketers and advertisers carefully design campaigns that tap into people's cravings and insecurities to promote their products, regardless of whether they are good for us. It is commonplace in the digital world for people to perpetuate stereotypes and misrepresentations. Certain ideas are brought to our attention while others are rarely mentioned, thereby influencing the agenda for our own thinking. All of these realities have potential spiritual implications, which is why I argue that life and faith in the digital age is an important topic for the church.

CRITICAL THINKING

When we watch a video online or consume some other sort of media, we rarely analyze the content. For many of us, this is a chance to stop thinking, to be entertained, to relax. Yet, it is during these informal times that ideas can ever so subtly find their way into our minds. But here's a question: without denying people a chance to relax and be entertained, how can we learn to be critical thinkers about the messages in our media? Part of the answer resides with a persistent and prayerful consideration of how the Ten Commandments apply to these new contexts, as we explored in chapter 16.

AN OPPORTUNITY TO EXPLORE SPIRITUAL THEMES

This is an exciting opportunity as well. Because media in the form of images and video in particular are such a large part of many people's lives, these media messages can be a starting point for discussions about matters of faith. We can turn this into an opportunity develop biblical perspective on many of the ideas and themes that come to us in the media.

EMPOWERING PEOPLE TO TAKE GREATER OWNERSHIP OF THEIR MEDIA DIET

More intentional conversations about media, its messages, and its influence are invitations for each of us to look at our own media diet and consider how it fuels our goals and values. Many of us are intentional with food, choosing to eat more of certain foods and less of others to achieve certain health goals. The same practice applies to the media we consume. How much do we consume? What is the nature of what we con-

57   Jason Lynch, "US Adults Consume an Entire Hour More Media Per Day," Adweek, June 27, 2016, http://www.adweek.com/tv-video/us-adults-consume-entire-hour-more-media-day-they-did-just-last-year-172218/ (accessed July 9, 2017).

sume? How does it affect the other things and people we value? How is it influencing us for better or worse?

A media diet is not a new concept. In fact, some might argue that it is a biblical one, going all the way back to the Old Testament times. The author of Ecclesiastes wrote, "My son, beware of anything beyond these. Of making many books there is no end, and much study is a weariness of the flesh" (12:12).

I once had a conversation with a parent who was very concerned about her daughter's media diet. Whenever there was a spare moment, the daughter turned to her phone, watching endless music videos and other videos about makeup. Over time, the daughter started to prefer watching these videos to family activities. Every car ride was a silent one as the daughter plugged in her headphones and listened to music. Even when doing homework, she needed frequent YouTube breaks before heading back to work. She spent hours each day on the screen, when only a couple of years before, she spent many of those hours engaged in family activities. The mother finally decided it was time for a break from the devices. The entire family took a break from screens for an entire week. They ate dinner together. They played board games. They talked. They went on walks. While there was no shortage of anger and tears at the beginning, by the end of the week, everyone talked about how much they enjoyed their time together. But the next week, the family returned to "normal."

This idea of thinking about media in terms of a diet can be helpful as it can help us think about how our use of media aligns with other goals and values in our lives. If we start from that perspective, then we can seek to use media in a way that aligns with our goals and values. Individually or as a family, we might choose to set some parameters for when, what, and how much we consume media so that we achieve our larger goals.

With this in mind, the following is a list of simple ways to increase our media literacy—to be more critical and discerning and to analyze and make sense of the messages we encounter. These techniques will help us assess and adjust our own approach to media. Finally, they will help us determine how to use media in positive ways, a topic we will examine in the next chapter.

Create and Discuss a Media Journal

For a few days or maybe even as long as a week, commit to keeping a journal of what media you consume, how much you consume, and when you consume it. You can also include short or quick reflections of why you consumed it and any initial thoughts about it. People vary as to how much time they spend on such a task, but simply trying this and gathering with others to discuss what you discovered can be enlightening. You could agree to do this as a family or with a friend.

The purpose of this activity is to help you become more aware of your media usage habits. Sometimes people are surprised to discover how much and how often they are online. People start to recognize what triggers heavier usage. Perhaps it's when they are stressed, bored, sick, tired, or upset about something; maybe other reasons will arise.

Debriefing about this experience is a chance for you to consider how your use of media aligns with your goals and values, how it influences your beliefs and values, and the extent to which it shapes what you think about throughout the day.

Interview People Who Work in Media to Learn How They Create Messages

There are countless online resources available if you want to learn how movies and television shows are made, how to create great video and images, and much more. Any of these can be useful starting points to introduce the fact that media creation is not a neutral exercise. People are incredibly thoughtful and intentional when they create messages, with the goal of emphasizing some things over others or promoting a certain feeling or experience over another. Learning about the mechanics of media creation can be both interesting and eye-opening for a family, class, or a small group in church.

Think about Bias

If you are creating a message or telling a story, you decide what to include and what to leave out. Even when you strive to be unbiased in your approach, your selection of what you focus upon and how you do so is, by nature, a form of bias. This is a reality of human limitation, and when it comes to media, it is a valuable lesson for us to remember.

A simple online search for "media bias" will result in thousands of interesting examples—and it takes time to vet those examples, first to see if they are true and accurate, and second to see if they are appropriate if you plan to share the information you discover with other people. Just identifying a few examples of media bias and discussing them together can help to develop media literacy. After going through such an activity, people tend to be a little more aware as they consume other media.

Look at Advertising

The Super Bowl is one of the most popular events on television each year, but not just for the game. The halftime show and commercials draw millions of viewers. Some consider advertising to be a form of art, given that it is a multibillion-dollar industry and garners awards and recognition. Companies do not spend hundreds of thousands and even millions of dollars on an advertisement and *hope* that they influence people. Advertising companies spending that much capital on one ad conduct ample research and carefully measure the return on their investments. They work hard to create memorable advertisements that improve awareness or opinion of their company or product and that influence consumers in ways that lead to increased sales.

This reality makes advertisements ideal examples to explore with your group as you talk about influence. Gather with a few people. Each of you can bring three to five examples of advertisements, then discuss them. Why do you like (or dislike) these particular ads? How do they work or influence people? Do we know if they work? What methods or messages do they use to influence consumers?

There are many information-rich books and resources about advertising. They share the history of advertising. They explain the theory that goes behind them, including no small amount of design theory and psychology. They share how marketers create them and how results are measured. In many congregations, you might also be able to find someone who works in marketing and advertising who would be willing to lead a discussion about how this works.

Study Music and Films

When I taught middle school and high school, I would have students identify their favorite or least favorite Christmas song during the season of Advent. Then, the class would listen to songs, study the lyrics, and discuss the meaning of the words. You can do the same thing with music and film, but, of course, film is more time-consuming. Like the world of advertising, film is an increasingly complex art and science, so finding a resource on filmmaking basics or bringing in a guest presenter to get you started can be helpful. Yet, taking the time to do so only helps you increase your media literacy and become more critical and discerning of the messages you encounter in daily life.

Evaluate Toys and Cartoons

Media and messages start early in a person's life, so we can also look at toy packaging, cartoons, and other media targeted at children. How are color and sound used to appeal to children? Who seems to be the target audience, and why? What are some of the intended messages? What are some of the subtle or unintended messages? What values and beliefs does the product or program highlight? If you do this with a group, you may ask that people also discuss whether the cartoon or the toy is appropriate for children in general or for children in the target age groups.

Evaluate the News

Earlier in the book, I mentioned a resource called *How to Watch the TV News* that is older but that I still find to be enlightening. This book gives a behind-the-scenes view of the news—what makes the cut, what does not, and why. You can even learn how camera angle, lighting, and other similar tools are used to communicate messages.

Learning about the news is helpful, but as with these other examples, it is beneficial to your group to watch it together and discuss what you are seeing and hearing. What topics or events do the news and media outlets highlight? What do they leave out? Do they accurately represent reality, or do they misrepresent it? How do they talk about morality and religion? You can certainly add your own questions as well. The goal of this exercise is to cultivate a more critical and discerning approach to news media.

Evaluate Photos and Illustrations

While video and audio are a large part of the modern world, still images are all around us, including billboards that line the highways, images everywhere we look online, and signs and visual messages posted throughout our communities. Any of these images provide an opportunity to analyze how they influence and what they communicate. If you conduct an online search for "images that changed the world," you will discover a number of impressive collections of images. Some websites even include commentary on each image. (If you are doing this exercise with young people, I urge you to preview and select the examples carefully, given that some examples are quite graphic.) You will learn about how photography helped the cause of the pro-life movement by sharing vivid images of unborn children. You will see how a photograph can increase awareness of injustice or cruelty in different parts of the world. You will see how photographs represent important moments in history. These are all useful ways to refine our visual literacy if we use them to think about the messages conveyed, what is not included, the benefits, and the limitations.

Track the Sources of Incorrect or Deceptive Media

There are many great online resources that offer examples of misleading photos, videos, and other media. This is further complicated by the fact that there are so many competing assessments of what people consider to be accurate or misleading.

If it aligns with our beliefs and values, we might be tempted to say that the message is accurate, but that is not always the case. Deceptive or misleading communication is not justified simply because it aligns with our personal beliefs. Remember: the end does not justify the means.

Compare How Different Sources Represent an Idea or Topic of Interest

I find great success in taking a topical approach, and there are different ways to do this. One is to compare how various media sources represent a specific topic or idea. You might choose a current topic of interest, one that is appropriate for the group you are working with. For example, some topics might be abortion, the role of religion in public life, immigration, war, the purpose of life, or poverty. After the topic is chosen, group members are charged with gathering examples of media treatment of that topic. In a simple show and tell, the group can discuss each example, looking at the different angles, biases, and messages represented.

Another approach is to choose a general social issue and try to get a sense of how media is influencing people's ideas about it. You might pick a theme such as racism, the role of women, the concept of marriage, the nature of family, the purpose of work, or the role of the government. The goal is to try to get a broad sense of how multiple media sources direct people's attention and influence public opinion. The group should be encouraged to candidly discuss how this influences us and our families.

Ask the Media Literacy Questions

The Center for Media Literacy is an online resource that provides a wealth of resources for teaching media literacy. Among them is a list of five simple questions worth asking when we "read" media. They are questions about authorship, format, audience, content, and purpose.

1. Who created this message?
2. What creative techniques are used to attract my attention?
3. How might other people understand this message differently from me?
4. What lifestyles, values, and points of view are represented in or omitted from this message?
5. Why is this message being sent?[58]

---

58 "Five Key Questions Form Foundation for Media Inquiry," Center for Media Literacy, http://www.medialit.org/reading-room/five-key-questions-form-foundation-media-inquiry (accessed March 19, 2017).

It is not easy to answer some of these questions. They force us to do some homework, and even then we may find it difficult. On occasion, I identify the author of the content and reach out directly. I am frequently and pleasantly surprised at how many of them respond. However, it is possible that some content creators are not fully aware of the messages and ideas they are communicating. Regardless, these five questions are a good and practical starting point as we try to refine our skills.

CONTRAST MEDIA MESSAGES WITH SCRIPTURE AND CHRISTIAN DOCTRINE

Many of the previous activities are useful for developing media literacy in ourselves and others, but those activities alone will not necessarily help us develop greater discernment about the messages and how they clash or align with Christian doctrine. For that, we must also add Scripture and other select resources to our reflections. There is a wealth of excellent Bible studies, topical texts on important social issues, and Bible commentaries that can be useful in this step of the process. Note that we are examining media while also turning to Scripture and vetted sources. In this way, we build our biblical and theological literacy while we develop discernment about how sources in the digital world represent those same ideas.

Discernment is not a skill we can develop in hours or days. It is a long-term and ongoing process. Because media messages come at us from all directions throughout all our lives, our goal now is to deepen our understanding of the Scriptures and Christian doctrine and to become increasingly skilled at analyzing the media around us through that biblical lens. It is fair to say that the task is never finished as long as we remain on earth, for it is a lifelong endeavor.

CREATE MESSAGES TOGETHER

Analyzing and discerning are good and important, but as I will argue further in the book, there are many opportunities to think about how we can be one of the many voices in the digital world. How can we add messages that others might find and consume? If more people are learning about truth claims, religious ideas, and moral truths through the many media and information sources available via the Internet—and if the creation and sharing of information and media is increasingly democratized, allowing almost anyone to contribute—then how might we contribute something positive, truthful, faithful, and God-pleasing? That is a question worth further investigation and consideration.

DISCUSSION AND REFLECTION QUESTIONS

- Which, if any, of the ideas in this chapter do you already use in your approach to analyzing media sources?

- Which of the ideas in this chapter resonate most with you, leading you to want to do something further in that area?

- Review the media literacy questions on page 126. How can you encourage yourself and others to use these in the consumption of media?

- How might you encourage yourself and others to explore what God's Word says about what we encounter in the media? List specific things you can do in your home, in your job, and in your church.

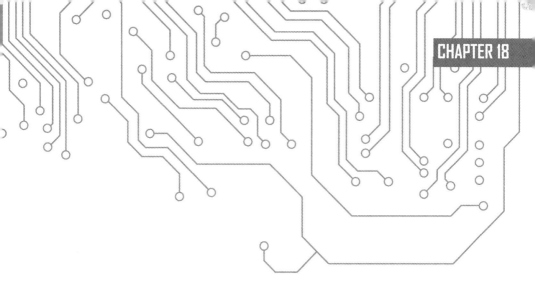

CHAPTER 18

Learning to Ask Questions

It was my first week as a middle school teacher, and we were assembling our students in the gymnasium for daily chapel. My group was seated right next to a colleague who, I soon learned, was truly a master educator. She had the ability to approach even the most challenging situations with a measure of calm and control, and her choice of words was so often perfect for the situation. The word that comes to mind when I think of her is *wise*. On this particular day, one of our energetic, curious sixth graders brought a tack to chapel, the kind used to put posters and other items on the bulletin boards in our classrooms. As you might expect, we teachers did not like the idea of a student bringing a tack to chapel. My colleague noticed it right away. She leaned over to him, looked him in the eyes, smiled, called him by name, and calmly asked a single question: "What good can come from bringing a tack to chapel?" I still remember the look on his face. It was a little blank. For a moment, it looked like he might try to justify his decision. But the question was just too good. He could not think of a reasonable answer. He reached out his hand and gave the tack to the teacher.

THE POWER OF A QUESTION

Questions are powerful. Unlike statements, they engage us. They require us to think or respond in some way, which is why they are a favorite tool of teachers and learners alike. I find that questions are valuable in exploring the nature of faith and life in the digital world. A single question can lead us into hours, days, or weeks of learning and reflecting. Questions help us get below the surface of things, to consider how something works or how it works on us. When I talk to people about how to prepare ourselves and others to make sense of this world, the art of learning to ask great questions is quite useful.

The Questions Jesus Asked

Because questions are a powerful teaching tool, it is no surprise that Jesus used them throughout His earthly ministry. For example, He asked many questions during His Sermon on the Mount. When teaching about loving our enemies, He asked, "And if you greet only your brothers, what more are you doing than others? Do not even the Gentiles do the same?" (Matthew 5:47). When teaching about worry, He offered a question for our consideration: "And which of you by being anxious can add a single hour to his span of life?" (6:27). When teaching about judging others, He asked, "Why do you see the speck that is in your brother's eye, but do not notice the log that is in your own eye?" (7:3). And when He talked about our Father's provision for us, He startled us with a direct question: "Which one of you, if his son asks him for bread, will give him a stone?" (7:9). We could go on for a long time listing examples of the questions Jesus asked. In my brief count of the number of questions Jesus asked as recorded in the Gospels, I stopped at just under three hundred. Interestingly, I found that He did not give answers to many of them. He merely asked questions, leaving His hearers to ponder and explore.

Jesus' questions stay with us. They invite us into a conversation and into reflection. They do not allow us to stop with simple and final answers. They invite us into something deeper. Along the way, we may find ourselves discovering things we never imagined.

The Postman Questions

Back in the 1990s, Postman's books revealed to me the world of media ecology,[59] challenged me to ask tough questions about our technological society, and introduced me to thinkers and authors such as Jacques Ellul, Lewis Mumford, Marshall McLuhan, and Walter Ong. These people come from different worldviews; not all of them approach the subject of technology from a distinctly Christian perspective. But their insights are useful in making us aware of the affordances and limitations of technology in society. More than anything, I appreciated a short list of questions that Postman asked students in a lecture at Calvin College to stimulate reflection on how a given technology uses or affects us.

---

59 Media ecology is a newer field focused upon the study of media, technology, and their effects on us and society. Postman was one of several formative voices in the field, helping to start the first PhD program in Media Ecology at New York University.

1. "What is the problem to which this technology is a solution?"[60]

Technology, by its nature and purpose, is about solving problems, even if it is a problem like "How do I come up with a game to overcome my boredom?" or "How do I make a game that is addictive and makes me lots of money?" Of course, there are more noble problems that people address with technology. For example, the Internet was created to solve a communication problem among researchers: "How can we leverage new knowledge about networks to share our research and ideas with one another across time and distance?"[61] We can ask this question of any technology. Finding the answer, however, is not always easy and may even be impossible. I have devoted more than two decades asking this question about technology in education and tracking down what seems to be the most likely answers. The answers are incredibly enlightening. Even seemingly mundane topics in education, when approached with this question, can take on the excitement and interest of the best mystery novels. For example, "What is the problem that the letter grade system in schools was created to solve?" "What is the problem that the multiple-choice test was created to solve?" "What is the problem that the use of bells in schools was created to solve?" You can ask similar questions about the technologies that are most deeply embedded in your life, and the journey to find the answers can be quite telling. In fact, you might sometimes discover that the original motivation for the technology's invention was less than impressive or favorable.

2. "Whose problem is it actually?"[62]

This is an equally fascinating question. Sometimes we find that it was a problem of a select few, but the solution applies to everyone. Alternatively, sometimes the solution serves some people well, but not necessarily others. The one-size-fits-all approach to problem-solving might be scalable, but how does it hold up if we are seeking to live out the command to love our neighbors, and those neighbors do not all have the same problems? There are, of course, some needs that we all share. Yet, when it comes to technologies, this question helps us reflect on whether a particular technology is indeed the best solution or whether alternatives might be more effective.

---

60   Neil Postman, "Technology and Society by Neil Postman," YouTube, July 17, 2007, https://youtu.be/uglSCuG31P4 (accessed March 19, 2017).

61   Barry Leiner et al., "Internet Society," Brief History of the Internet—Internet Timeline, http://www.internetsociety.org/internet/what-internet/history-internet/brief-history-internet (accessed March 19, 2017).

62   Postman, "Technology and Society," YouTube.

3. "If there is a legitimate problem that is solved by the technology, what other problems will be caused by my using this technology?"[63]

This question brings us to the heart of the affordances and limitations concept to which I keep referring. When we come up with a solution to a problem, it may well solve that problem, but it may also create other problems. The automobile solved many problems related to transportation. It also created jobs and expanded our ability to travel further distances on our own. But it also had negative results, such as traffic jams, traffic accidents, and pollution. With technology, we weigh the potential benefits against the potential downsides.

We do not always anticipate the problems caused by our solutions. We tend to focus on the solutions so much that we ignore or forget that we risk creating new or even greater problems. While it is impossible to anticipate every possible new problem generated by a technology, the exercise of thinking through what we create and use allows us to try to resolve potential problems before we create the technology. This question can also help us to decide if and how to use a specific technology when it becomes available to us.

When my daughter was an infant, she was a light sleeper. Any sound would wake her. She was almost two years old before she slept through the night. Some people insisted that if we just acclimated her to sounds, she would get used to it; but after weeks of trying with our sleep deprivation growing, we gave up. We opted for a different solution. We turned off the ringers on the phones, sending everything to voicemail. (We actually liked life in a home without a half dozen calls in the evening). While we did not get to pick up the phone when family members and friends called, a flashing light on the phone alerted us to a message. We checked the messages a couple times a day and returned calls when necessary. I realized how conditioned we had become to run to the phone whenever it rang. The phone had taken precedence over family conversations and other activities. But not so with our new practice. We came to like it so much that we continued it for a year or two after our daughter began sleeping better.

This example helps to explain that there are benefits and limitations to every technology, but we get so used to them in our lives, maybe even learning to accept, like, or at least tolerate the downsides, that we stop being aware of them. I have come to appreciate making conscious choices—more thoughtful and deliberate decisions about how and why to use a technology. By doing so, we create opportunities for important conversations in our family about our vocations, values, and priorities and how we can

---

63   Ibid.

shape our technology use to support those goals. I contend this is a useful exercise for the home, the church, and our personal lives as well.

LEARNING TO ASK QUESTIONS

4. "Am I using this technology or is it using me?"[64]

This last question surfaces all sorts of interesting insights. For example, we are always using technology in some way. Perhaps we are required to use it for work, school, or another context. Or perhaps a technology is just part of life in the modern world. I might choose whether to use a car if I lived in New York City, where there is ample public transportation; but if I live in a rural community and my work requires some measure of travel, I have fewer options.

Consider the cell phone. Some people have a job that requires them to be available in the evenings or on the weekends, and the existence of the cell phone drives the growth of such expectations. In other situations, we have a choice about the kind of phone we use. Yet, the moment we start to use a technology like a cell phone, we tend to let it use us as well. We set alerts so we are notified each time we get a phone call, a voicemail, an email, a notification on social media, a text message, a weather update, or a new deal at Starbucks. We can turn off the alerts, limit how often we check our messages, and delete apps that distract us. However, if our default approach is to accept all that a cell phone offers and adapt our lives to all its options, then that technology (or in the case of a cell phone, that collection of technologies) uses us.

I once talked to a friend who shared that her congregation assembled a committee to discuss the role of email in the church. What are its benefits and limitations? What guidelines might the committee suggest for when to use email, whether to use it, and how to use it? Did the committee want to work through major issues via email, or did they recommend face-to-face conversations on certain matters? What fascinated me about this is that this congregation's leaders recognized that a technology such as email has both affordances and limitations. They understood that it solved some problems and created others. They also understood that their decision was not just a matter of using a technology, but that the technology could begin to shape or reshape the way they functioned as a community. They wanted to maintain their values, so they assembled a group to prayerfully consider the possibilities and make recommendations to the congregation. This is an excellent example of thoughtful and deliberate living in the digital world. Instead of just following wherever the technology would lead them, they paused, considered, studied, prayed, and decided from there.

---

64   Ibid.

In another example, I spoke to a church that was struggling with whether to put a projection screen in their sanctuary. There was no small measure of disagreement about it, so I suggested Postman's four questions as a starting point. Of course, there were many other questions they asked as well, but even the first question made for a good and important conversation in their congregation. It forced them to examine their motives and goals and prompted them to think about other solutions that might be more effective in achieving those goals. The question about whose problem it was provided them with an opportunity to listen and learn from one another's challenges, concerns, and questions. The process of questioning and deciding on a solution is more significant to our conversation here than the congregation's final choice because they learned many important things in the process of discussing these questions together, seeking biblical wisdom, praying together, and caring for the needs of one another.

This is a reason why a simple list of what to do and not to do regarding various technologies in church and home is not, in my opinion, helpful. Rather, the value lies in the process of asking these questions together and seeking answers individually and as a community. Such an exercise is too valuable to bypass with a list of do or don't statements that might or might not be applicable in a given context.

QUESTIONS TO UNDERSTAND

Notice how the Postman questions are really an invitation to seek greater and deeper understanding. Where we end up matters. But the journey itself matters as well. Much of the growth, learning, and perspective comes out of that journey—especially as we take those steps with others.

QUESTIONS TO CHANGE OUR PERSPECTIVES

From the two examples I just provided, you can see how asking these questions helps us to change our perspective and to understand the perspective of others. This is especially important in an age when messages can be deceptive. If we are not careful, we can easily misread intentions and motives, misinterpret what is being communicated, or misunderstand the goal of a given technology.

I learned this when talking to a young man who lived in a high crime, low income community and spent almost every night on the computer. He was spending almost forty hours a week on a computer. When I first learned this, my initial reaction was, I admit, judgmental. Why are people letting him sit at a computer for so long? Instead of voicing that, however, I asked him to tell me more. I learned about his family situation, and the fact that his parents were not in the home. His caregiver, who was ill, did not want him to leave the house because she was concerned for his safety. The Internet was the means by which he connected with friends and with a sibling who lived in a different city. The Internet was his connection to people. If I had given in to judgment, I would have missed learning about his story, which was key to assessing his situation.

We all hang on to stereotypes and make assumptions. By starting with questions and curiosity, we test those assumptions while getting to know other people. We are able to develop insight and perspective that are important in loving the neighbors around us and releasing our hold on stereotypes.

QUESTIONS TO INVITE CONVERSATION

Postman's questions also create opportunities for useful conversations in which multiple people share ideas and insights. People learn from one another. They come together to work through biblical insights on how they might best proceed. We learn as we discuss, which is why we are advised to talk about the Ten Commandments with others as we go about our lives (Deuteronomy 6:1–9).

QUESTIONS TO CHALLENGE

In James 1:2–4, we are told, "Count it all joy, my brothers, when you meet trials of various kinds, for you know that the testing of your faith produces steadfastness. And let steadfastness have its full effect, that you may be perfect and complete, lacking in nothing." That passage appears to be speaking to trials in our lives, but it is not much of a stretch to recognize how questions offer us a different type of challenge or trial. Challenges help us grow. A carefully considered question challenges our current way of thinking and helps us consider what we do not yet know. It has the potential to both humble us and inspire us to seek out what we do not yet have.

QUESTIONS FOR SELF-REFLECTION

When I was a new teacher, I asked myself ten to fifteen questions at the end of every week. I asked these questions, for example:

- Is there a student who is in special need of prayer?

- Are there students who struggle more than others? If so, how can I help?

- Which students are thriving? How can I encourage them?

- Do I have sins to confess about how I treated my students this week?

- Were my students engaged or disengaged this week? Why?

Over the years, I revised my list, but these questions offered me a chance to reflect on my context and on myself. On more than a few occasions, these questions helped me recognize my shortfalls, my sins, and where I needed to change or grow. Sometimes I turned to a trusted colleague or my pastor for further help. This was an important part of my growth and formation as a teacher.

The same thing can occur for all of us as we examine our lives in this digital world. The questions will not be the same, but asking challenging questions about our digital lives and decisions and then taking time for genuine reflection is important. We become distracted by the busyness of life and the demands that pull us in different directions—traps of this modern age. There is the equal danger that we become so caught up in self-reflection that we fail to look outward and upward. The psalmist describes it this way: "Blessed is the man who walks not in the counsel of the wicked, nor stands in the way of sinners, nor sits in the seat of scoffers; but his delight is in the law of the LORD, and on His law he meditates day and night" (Psalm 1:1–2). He does not just sit in his bed meditating upon himself and his questions; he mediates on the law of the Lord.

As we consider these hard questions and allow ourselves to honestly assess the place of technology in our lives, we are continually reminded of God's unchanging nature, His love for us, and His grace in His Word and Sacraments. There we discover the strength, courage, and purpose to continue with our questions about our lives in the digital world today. It is only in God's Word and Sacraments that we find God's grace. We learn of God's unchanging nature and His love for us, and there, we discover the strength, courage, and purpose to continue with our questions about life today.

DISCUSSION AND REFLECTION QUESTIONS

- How often do you take the time to ask the sort of questions mentioned in this chapter? What other important questions would you ask and encourage others to ask?

- As we reflect upon Jesus' example, what lessons can we apply to the importance of questions for our faith and life in the digital world?

- When talking to people about the challenges of Christian life in the digital age, questions can be a great way to promote discussion. Think of a challenge that is especially important to you, one that has been inaugurated by the digital age. List three to five questions you might ask to spark a positive conversation about that topic.

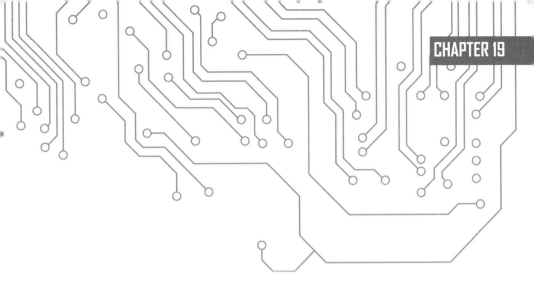

CHAPTER 19

Creation and Communication vs. Distant Criticism

In much of this book, I argue that it is important to develop critical thinking skills and discernment about faith and life in the digital world. Part of the purpose of that is so we are not misled or drawn away from God's Word by the world in which we live. It is not just a negative and reactive response, however. It is also about coming to understand that, as Christians, we control how we respond to the world around us. In many instances, we make choices about which technologies we use and which ones we do not. We make decisions about how we use them. Yet, there is still another reason why this examination has value: we have an opportunity to be witnesses in this digital realm, just as we can be in all other areas of our lives.

When Jesus first spoke the words of the Great Commission (Matthew 28:18–20), no one who heard Him could have imagined that "all nations" would include virtual worlds and digital spaces, but that is where people today are spending their time. The agora of ancient Greece, where early Christians witnessed, has moved to the digital realm today, at least in part. It is the modern-day gathering place. More ideas are spread and exchanged there than anywhere else. It is a truly global exchange of ideas.

Earlier in the book, I mentioned my amazement at the connections that resulted when I created a simple blog and started sharing my ideas. Blogging, for me, is just writing a rough draft of my thoughts and inviting anyone and everyone to join me for a digital cup of coffee to chat about them. What is still baffling to me is that my visitor statistics show that people from all over the world are reading my blog. What follows is an excerpt from a blog post I wrote in early 2017:

I counted twice on this one because I did not believe the results at first. Out of the 196 countries in the world, people from 185 of those countries read one or more articles on Etale in 2016. English-speaking countries are obviously at the top of the list. The largest number of readers in 2016 came from the United States. After that, there was a close second between Canada, Australia, the United Kingdom, and India. Then there is a third grouping that included the European Union, the Philippines, New Zealand, Hong Kong, South Africa, Malaysia, and Singapore. The fourth group included Pakistan along with individual naming of most of the countries in the European Union (I am not quite sure about the rhyme or reason behind some visitors showing up by a specific country and others simply by the broader "European Union" label).[65]

People from all but eleven of the world's countries visited my blog in 2016. I write quite a bit, up to three articles a week, but I had no idea that what I wrote could possibly reach that many people. This compels me to dedicate this chapter to what I see as an incredible opportunity. So, this chapter is more than a challenge to analyze life in the digital world. It's a challenge to become creating and contributing members in the global digital landscape.

While this might be beyond the comfort zone of some readers, I suggest there is value in thinking about how we can be present in and contributing members of the digital world. I will expand on this in the next chapter, but here we will focus on simple ways that we can think about being a voice and a witness as we go about our lives, including the digital elements of our lives. This is a far from exhaustive list, but this chapter consists of a few ideas for your consideration.

WHAT YOU WRITE

Most of us use email and texting, and many of us post at least occasional messages on one or more social media sites. With email, we are typically writing to a single person or to a small group of people. Email is the letter of the present age, at least for most people. This kind of communication informs and influences people, and what we say in our emails can be both a blessing and a curse to others. How can we, even in subtle ways, embrace the command to love our many neighbors in the world by what

---

65   Bernard Bull, "Etale Year in Review—185 countries, 185 articles, Top Articles, Top Searches, and More," *Etale*, December 28, 2016, http://etale.org/main/2016/12/29/top-10-etale-articles-of-2016/ (accessed March 19, 2017).

we write? I offer this as a question for your reflection, not to be prescriptive. I will also share some of my own reflections about where I have been and where I am now.

When I reply to people via email, unless it is a rapid or ongoing exchange of messages, I try to begin by recognizing them by name and more often than not thanking them in some way. This is not just some proper etiquette rule that I am trying to follow. I am genuinely grateful for their time and attention. Out of all the things that could occupy their time, they chose to share at least a small portion of it with me, so I thank them for their message.

After that, I try to attend to the purpose of their email, answering questions to the best of my ability. As I answer, I strive to avoid potential misunderstandings. If I suspect there is an emotional element at work in some way, or if there is a risk of confusion, I suggest that we discuss it in person or via phone, so even if I cannot see them face-to-face, I can at least hear the tone of their voice, something that is lost in email. Sometimes I even suggest one of the many free video conferencing options so we can look each other in the eyes as we speak.

Sometimes I have an emotional reaction to an email; perhaps I am initially offended by how or what they write. I might find myself feeling angry, sad, or frustrated. When that happens, writing back immediately is not always the wisest idea. I might respond immediately to acknowledge receipt, but I hold off to provide a more substantive reply or ask for an in-person meeting.

As I conclude my emails, I often finish with an offer of God's blessings to the person. While I acknowledge the risk of such an ending sounding insincere or used without consideration for its true meaning, many people find it refreshing and encouraging to have someone write candidly about matters of faith. Similarly, if there are any personal concerns or struggles that people mention in an email, I try to take note of them, pause for an immediate prayer, and then let them know I am praying for them.

There is nothing earth shattering about these small acts, but God calls us to love our neighbors, and I think about how I might do that even through quick email exchanges. Even as I write this, I do it with a small measure of concern about the many times I did not do these things in previous emails. I am far from perfect, and I do not always practice what I preach. Yet, this is what I seek to do out of a genuine interest in others.

One of my more embarrassing failures in this regard occurred more than a decade ago. I was new at my place of work and still learning to work well with a colleague who is now one of my closest and most trusted partners in my work. At the time, however, I was frustrated with something that had happened. I do not remember what, but I wrote a three-thousand-word email, full of my concerns and complaints. I sent it on a Friday evening, and I included two other people on the email who did not need to be involved. This was a selfish act. Not once did I think about love of my neighbor while I crafted that email. I wanted to get everything out before the weekend so I could stop thinking about it, even though I was putting the burden on the others in the email chain. I disrespected the main recipient and escalated the tension by copying the other people. There are so many ill-informed and misguided elements of that email I could point to, and that is why I include it as an illustration. That email did not reflect the lessons I am trying to teach here about loving our neighbors, for I used my writing that Friday evening to curse, not to bless.

I recognized my wrong in the situation and sought forgiveness from the associated parties; they graciously forgave me. We all learned from that exchange, and our working relationship improved significantly. I share this as a classic example of the dangers of digital communication and losing sight of the people on the other side of the email.

Email is one thing. What about the many messages that we share on social media? Each message we share via social media is an opportunity to love our neighbors. We see people practicing this. Some are intentional about sharing inspirational quotes and Bible verses. Others intentionally use the platform to offer encouragement to other people.

There are many possibilities for creating content that blesses others. However, what I consider most important is that we make deliberate choices about how we represent ourselves as followers of Christ through the messages we create and the content we share or endorse.

What is the equivalent for you? I invite you to consider how email and other digital messages can be opportunities to love the neighbors who will read or receive your messages, whether text messages, emails, or social media posts you share with family, friends, co-workers, and others.

What You Model

A new platform takes us out of our routine thoughts, actions, and habits. We may find ourselves doing things that we might not consider doing in any other place. That is why it is necessary to move from spontaneous, knee-jerk responses to more deliberate and prayerful ones. People see what we write, how we represent ourselves, and the sources and ideas we endorse. This communicates a great deal to others, often more than we realize. It is helpful not only to be deliberate and thoughtful, but also to seek counsel and feedback from others. What we perceive of how we represent ourselves is not always how others perceive us.

For example, a manager used to send out daily electronic messages to the rest of her unit at work. She tried hard to be positive, creating a comfortable and light-hearted environment. She loved cats, so one way she thought to be more informal and light-hearted was to phonetically spell out cat sounds in her emails. If she liked something, she would write as much and follow it with "prrrrrrrrr." She thought this was funny and friendly. Even reading this, you might be thinking otherwise. A colleague finally pulled her aside and explained that including cat sounds in her messages was undermining the respect others had for her. People did not receive this as friendly and light-hearted; they thought it was unprofessional and strange. It was a complete surprise to her when she heard this.

That might seem like an extreme example. However, there are plenty of others that are less extreme but just as significant. There is the pastor who posts about his strong political convictions on social media, unknowingly creating a barrier between himself and members who have different political viewpoints. There is the person who comes across as angry or complaining but is, in her mind, trying to be funny. There is the person who loves to share ideas, but does not realize he sounds arrogant. There is the person who unknowingly shares false news. There is the one who gossips, but does not recognize it as such.

The point is that social media is like a different culture (or maybe a collection of subcultures). Our comments that are received well in face-to-face situations may not transfer well to the digital world, so we are called to constantly learn how to communicate clearly and effectively in these forums, and how to manifest our beliefs and values consistently in these spaces.

Creation over Critique

Another important point here has to do with whether we choose to engage the digital world as critics and consumers or as creators. Part of what we create might be our participation in social media outlets by the types of messages we share with others. The digital world is like a mass of bustling cities worthy of interaction, and for the person who is willing, there are countless opportunities to be a positive influence. In the next chapter, we will examine a variety of ways to do just that.

DISCUSSION AND REFLECTION QUESTIONS

- When it comes to faith and life in the digital world, do you find yourself engaged more in creation or in critique? Explain.

- How do you or could you go about prayerfully and thoughtfully creating messages to share with others in the digital world?

- How might you engage in more creation? These need not be major projects. Also think about small things you can do with minimal effort.

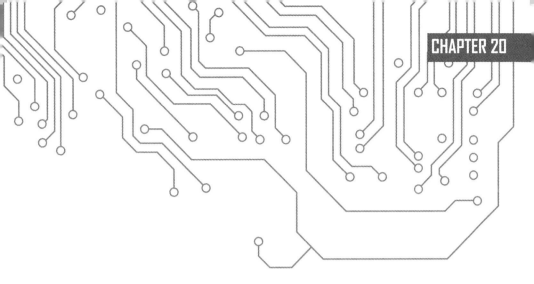

CHAPTER 20

Engagement in the Digital World

When I speak to groups, I share many of the ideas mentioned in this book, and I also invite them to think about how they might engage people in the digital world, seeking opportunities to build relationships, be a Christian witness, and live out one or more of their vocations. This is what I want to focus on now. How can we be a positive influence in the digital world?

To begin, I find it helpful to describe three categories, or types, of engagement. Some may be of more interest to you than others. Many of these are things you can do as a church, but some individuals also get involved with them. The first is relating to people in the digital world. The second is what I call preparing for battle. The third is becoming a more active and engaged member of the digital world.

RELATING TO PEOPLE IN THE DIGITAL WORLD

A book called *Peace Child* offers a powerful lesson about connecting with people.[66] In this book, a man is the first missionary sent to a small people group in the Irian Jaya of Papua New Guinea. The missionary faced no small number of challenges. He had to learn a new language, learn the culture, build relationships, and acclimate to a new physical environment. This particular people group also observed a tradition of cannibalism.

The missionary arrived and spent quite some time with the people. He was excited to make progress toward sharing the story of Jesus. But when Holy Week arrived, he ran into a major problem. As the missionary shared the story Judas betraying Jesus with

---

66   Don Richardson, *Peace Child* (Minneapolis: Bethany House, 2014).

a kiss, there was a strange excitement in the group. The people regarded Judas as a hero.

Now that is a major worldview collision. Jesus was a character they laughed at while Judas was the hero, a response deeply embedded into their culture. As I mentioned, this group had a tradition of cannibalism, but not some sort of random act of killing and eating other people. Instead, one villager would befriend someone from another village. They would build that relationship and the trust over an extended period. Then, when there was adequate trust, they would invite the friend to dinner. Little did that friend know that this was the grand deception, leading to his death and consumption. To the people in this village who were learning about the life of Jesus, Judas was the brilliant mastermind of a respected deception and betrayal.

In addition to this situation, the villages frequently battled one another, so personal safety was a consideration. How could this missionary possibly get through to a people who not only think Judas is a hero but also are in constant feuds? The missionary didn't know, so he announced to the villagers that he and his wife planned to leave.

The people did not want him to leave, so they did something to prevent it. They sought to make peace between the warring villages. Given their long-held traditions of feuding, how do they make peace? Within their culture, the people could create a type of treaty. It involved what they referred to as a "peace child." Members of one village would give a child to members of another village. This exchanging of children connected the villages, building trust and bringing about peace.

Seeing this act of sacrificing one's son for the sake of peace was an epiphany for the missionary. He decided to stay. As he retold the story of Jesus, he explained that Jesus is like God's peace child. The missionary used this as a comparison, even if not a perfect one, to share the unchanging truth of the Gospel. And over time, God worked through His Word to bring many to faith. In fact, the church established by the people in that community is still active more than fifty years later.[67]

There are many lessons that can be gleaned from this story, but for our purpose, it is a helpful example of finding something within a culture that can help you better communicate the unchanging Gospel message with others. We see Jesus do this in His parables as He told stories using characters and events familiar to His audience. Jesus used the familiar to teach an important truth. His parables were about shepherds, farmers, and vineyards, things His audience knew well.

A fundamental lesson about teaching is that the better you know your audience,

---

67   David Ranish, "Fifty years later, 'Peace Child' tribe still following Christ," *Mission Network News*, https://www.mnnonline.org/news/fifty-years-later-peace-child-tribe-still-following-christ/ (accessed March 19, 2017).

the more easily you will be able to help them connect with your message. Therefore, one approach to digital ministry is simply getting to know what is going on in the digital world. We then use information about digital culture to create illustrations and examples that will help our learners. We may not actually use digital tools or get involved in the digital world, but we might create a lesson about how being connected to God is like having an unlimited cell phone plan. We might then explain that connectivity with God is so much better. This sort of teaching, where we use examples from the lives of listeners, is what Jesus did. Maybe the cell phone example is too cliché, but there are countless others. As we listen, observe, and learn, we will discover new analogies and illustrations.

When I first started teaching middle school, I wanted to help students get a biblical perspective on the many ideas they garnered from various media sources. This was in the 1990s, so I started by asking students about what they liked to read. I gathered a short list of popular magazines such as *Teen Magazine, CosmoGirl, MAD Magazine, Sports Illustrated,* and *Rolling Stone.* Every few weeks I spent a couple of hours at the local library scanning the headlines and articles. I found articles offering advice on countless topics, and while the advice was sometimes benign, it was just as often troubling and misleading.

I used the headlines as conversation starters in my classes. I started with the questions and topics addressed in the magazines, but then invited students to join me in exploring what the Scriptures teach us about the topics addressed in the various publications. These were some of the richest and most rewarding teaching moments of my early years in the classroom. Students were interested in these topics. I did not always tell them where I found the topics, but when I brought them up, I could see heads perk up since these topics, prompted by their recent reading, were fresh in their minds.

Just as often, I would learn about stories and examples in these magazines that I could use to teach a different truth. For example, I would introduce a *Sports Illustrated* story about an athlete who faced some adversity and use that as a starting point to teach the Bible lesson for the day.

We can do this same thing in our homes, churches, schools, and jobs. Instead of magazine articles, we might begin with some aspect of their digital lives and interests. We can use these as discussion starters for what can turn into wonderfully meaningful conversations and opportunities to share our faith. Within the context of church and home, this is also a great way to initiate the faith conversations about digital life that I keep encouraging throughout this book.

However, there is a risk of going too far. In 1 Corinthians 2:4, Paul explains that his message was not "in plausible words of wisdom, but in demonstration of the Spirit and of power." God's Word does not need us to dress it up in fancy cultural jargon for it to accomplish its purpose. We want to communicate in ways that are understandable to people. Language and culture are deeply intertwined. In addition, we want to avoid binging on all things digital and technological with the simple justification that we are doing it so that we can be better witnesses. There are obvious limits to that perspective. What I am suggesting is that we return to the example of Paul in Athens when he listened and learned from the world around him and then used what he learned to be a witness for the Gospel.

PREPARING FOR BATTLE

Paul wrote, "For we do not wrestle against flesh and blood, but against the rulers, against the authorities, against the cosmic powers over this present darkness, against the spiritual forces of evil in the heavenly places" (Ephesians 6:12). This second approach to engagement takes us a step further. Not only do we get to know the digital world, but we also make a concerted effort to help others analyze it from the viewpoint of God's Word. We then go even further; we make it our mission to prepare and equip ourselves and others with what we need to stand firm in the faith amid the challenges and opportunities of the world today. This focus asks one main question: How can I apply God's Word to life in the digital world? Again, the answer may not come in the form of a simple list of dos and don'ts. This is a continuous challenge, but a good and important one. It is one that leads us to have those ongoing conversations with friends, family, and others in our churches. As each new development arises, we study God's Word anew for guidance on how we might respond.

This second approach stems from the first part of the book, where I outlined a few cultural shifts that have emerged, at least in part, because of digital culture. The digital world is not neutral; it is laden with values. What happens when innovations, technologies, and aspects of digital culture merge into our lives, our families, our churches, and our communities? They amplify certain values while muffling others. There might not always be a definitive right or wrong, but there are always important questions for us to consider.

A Christian worldview guides us in navigating such a world. Consider the example of innovations in the healthcare fields. When the possibility of stem cell research emerged, some in the scientific community jumped at the opportunity to study embryonic stem cells with limited consideration for moral implications. Is an embryonic stem cell a human life worthy of protection, or should researchers disregard such questions for the sake of what they deem the greater good? Christians played an important role in raising this question and forcing more candid dialogue about this important issue. They also argued that it is important to consider the comparative benefits of adult stem cell research as an alternative.

Countless values-laden issues exist in the broader digital and technological world today. When some are so focused upon progress as the ultimate goal, with an end-justifies-the-means moral compass, people of faith play an important role in these conversations. If we are silent, we may find ourselves eventually living in a society where standing up for our beliefs and moral convictions will put us in conflict with the law. In reality, even if we speak up, we may find that to be the case. This is certainly true when it comes to life issues, Christian values about marriage and family, and the implications of living in a nation where we value freedom of religion. Nonetheless, speaking up and standing up for our Christian convictions is our calling. Even when we lack clarity about the issues, we can play a role in promoting important discussion. Now, drawing from earlier chapters of this book, I offer a summary of some of the many emerging areas where a Christian worldview offers an important voice in the larger discussion. I also invite you to add to this list.

Sinful Nature

The idea that each of us is born sinful is not a popular one in the contemporary world. Some argue that people are born basically good, though perhaps tainted by a corrupt society. Some argue that people are born neither good nor evil. Still others deny the idea of evil altogether. Scripture, on the other hand, is clear. We are indeed born sinful. Left to our own means, we persistently demonstrate a propensity toward making things worse, not better. As the psalmist explains in Psalm 51:5, "Behold, I was brought forth in iniquity, and in sin did my mother conceive me."

In Genesis 11:1–9, we discover one example of what happens when people grow in their capacity for communication and collaboration toward a shared goal. While we can recognize, celebrate, and benefit from using digital tools for new types of collaboration, we also know from the Tower of Babel account that people do not always use such capabilities for good. We just as often find ourselves using new technologies and capacities to disregard our need for God. We fall into the age-old trap of convincing ourselves that we do not need a Savior.

In such times, Christians have the opportunity to offer a clear, simple, and winsome response to such utopian visions. Again, we do not need to throw out everything or come off as the persistent naysayer of technological benefits. We can celebrate the benefits while also reminding ourselves, our family, and others about our need for something greater.

Narcissism

Look at the names of products and services in this age, and we see "I" at the fore. More than any other time in history, we live in an individualized, personalized, and customized world. We can celebrate some of the benefits that come with this. In education, for example, we as Christians are the first to recognize that each student is a unique creation of God. God calls each person to a variety of vocations. We celebrate how we can use new technologies and resources to fulfill these vocations and nurture the unique gifts, talents, abilities, and callings of learners. Yet, we do so in a way that does not elevate the learner as the center of the universe. Education equips us for service to God and neighbor. It is not all about the "I" or "you." This same thing holds true beyond education. We find it in entertainment, healthcare, and much of the service industry today.

One of the things we as Christians offer to such a world is a reminder that this world is not all about us and that there is a serious risk in a world of "I." In the ancient Greek myth of Narcissus, we learn about a man known for his beauty. People all around him admired him for it. His preoccupation also became his demise. Looking into a pool of water, Narcissus fell in love with his own reflection. He became so fixated on his own appearance that he lost sight of even his basic needs, eventually dying because of his self-absorption.

This is not a new danger to us as Christians. The Scriptures warn us of it often. We know that the self is always drawing us away from the wisdom of the First Commandment. Life becomes increasingly shallow when we come to believe that its greatest end is personal satisfaction and self-actualization, being catered to by a world of personalization, individualization, and customization. That does not mean that it is wrong to celebrate and benefit from some aspects of such a world, but there are clear risks, and the Scriptures offer us a worldview that puts God at the center, not humanity or our personal needs, desires, and goals.

Consider the profound truths in Matthew 22:36–40. A man asks Jesus about the greatest commandment. Jesus replied, "You shall love the Lord your God with all your heart and with all your soul and with all your mind. This is the great and first commandment. And a second is like it: You shall love your neighbor as yourself. On these two commandments depend all the Law and the Prophets." Both commandments are outward focused. Our purpose does not focus upon meeting personal needs but upon something outside of us. Even our salvation comes from outside of us: "There is salvation in no one else, for there is no other name under heaven given among men by which we must be saved" (Acts 4:12).

The Search for Eternity

As already examined, there is a growing desire to manufacture eternity through technological advancement. More than twenty years ago, when I first started teaching, I attended a public school conference where the keynote speaker boasted of a future where we would eventually solve the problem of death. He mused about a time when humans will overcome the physiological problem of death or will create a disembodied eternity in cyberspace. We are nearing a time, he mused, when those who are near death will upload their consciousness into the Internet and live forever. This might sound like something out of a science fiction film or book, but these are the dreams of some people today. Even those who do not go to such extremes find themselves placing even greater hope in the promise of technology.

We have an important alternative message to share in such a world. Death is not the end that some fear. The Scriptures teach us about the promise of eternal life made possible in Jesus Christ. As has always occurred, some will dismiss such a message, but in the context of these contemporary dreams and musings about life and death, Christians have a greater message of hope and truth to share.

Human Progress

The technocratic worldview is one of progress. There is a relentless bias toward new and better. Newer cars are better. Newer homes are better. Newer devices are better. The lifespan of many technologies is only a few years. This keeps us wanting and buying something more, better, newer. And if we don't have the latest gadget, some might even experience guilt, jealousy, or even worse—the feeling of being behind the times (what some may call the "fear of missing out").

There is a limitation to this worldview. Christianity is a historic religion, rooted in actual events that occurred in the past. God actually created the world and humanity. He actually sent His Son, who lived, died, and rose again from the dead. We believe in the importance of the past and recognize that new is not always better. We also recognize that, as much as we might appreciate progress in terms of scientific knowledge and technological applications, the effects of sin have always been pervasive in our world and our lives. Even when we think we are making great progress, we realize that, over time, sin is eating away at the world. There is no series of human innovations that will place us in an ideal and utopian world. The only central moment in the future that leads to true newness is the return of Jesus Christ.

EFFICIENCY

Efficiency is another value inherent in most technologies. The goal is to do things better and faster and with less waste. These can be good and noble efforts indeed. If we can find better ways to care for the less fortunate, by all means, we should do so. At the same time, efficiency is not the ultimate end in every situation. There are times when other values are more appropriately elevated above efficiency. We have ample examples of this in the Scriptures. The Israelites did not travel in the most efficient way through the wilderness. The missionaries of the New Testament did not always break down every missionary journey into systematic and strategic quadrants. There are many other potential values that play a more important role in our lives, families, and churches than efficiency. Even as some champion efficiency as the ultimate aim in our society, there are times when we appropriately offer different ways to approach matters.

QUANTIFICATION

We live in a world of big data and analytics. We document every one of our actions online. Students in schools are rated, graded, and tested. We seek easy numbers to quantify our progress toward goals and milestones. In a digital world where everything can be reduced to ones and zeros, rating, ranking, and quantifying are at the top of many priority lists. As Christians, we can celebrate the gift of math and numbers and seek to use them in service to our neighbor. Yet, the Scriptures offer us a worldview that goes far beyond quantification. People are more than numbers. Our families and churches are more than numbers. Our Christian schools and other organizations are as well. This does not mean that we cannot learn from aspects of society that are driven by numbers, but there is more to what we do, why we do it, and how we do it.

This is no small matter today, as pure quantification risks minimizing important aspects of faith and life. We face the danger of being sidetracked by trying to quantify things instead of investing in priorities that are more important. Again, numbers are a blessing and can play a role, but a Christian worldview offers a much more holistic view of life. In fact, I contend that this perspective is one that Christians have the opportunity to bring with them amid many vocations. A Christian working in healthcare can embrace the opportunities of health informatics. A teacher might celebrate the chance to use numeric data to analyze student needs and help them learn. A businessperson might seek to analyze data so that he or she can better serve clients or customers while also maintaining good stewardship. There are plenty of other possibilities. At the same time, we know there is much more to the command to love our neighbor, and we are conscious of the dangers associated with letting our priorities be sidetracked by a singular focus on numbers.

COMMUNITY

As much as we can celebrate the promise and possibility of online communication, collaboration, and community, there is another important perspective for us to consider. God's plan to address the problem of sin in the world did not involve a virtual or symbolic sending of a Savior. It involved the incarnation, God in the flesh. This is a grand and incredible aspect of God's plan, that Jesus was born as a baby, fully man and fully God. He did not consider a virtual visit, a remote call, or a hologram adequate for His purposes. When Jesus healed the man with leprosy, He ignored the customs of the day that said to avoid lepers physically. Even before healing the man's ailment, Jesus touched him (Matthew 8:3). We also know about the Early Church tradition of greeting one another with a "holy kiss" (Romans 16:16). In each of these examples, we find that physical presence and touch played an important role.

I do not mean to suggest that virtuality is wrong or that online and remote communication is sinful. What I offer, however, is an important balance to our growing celebration and use of the virtual, remote, and online. While there is nothing prescriptive in Scripture on this matter, we do see throughout Scripture that there is value in the physical aspect of connections and interactions. How can and should this inform our decisions as Christians? That is an important question for us today. We must beware of legalism and forcing our instincts upon others, but we are also wise to consider the tension between the value of physical interaction and the virtual interactions that will become increasingly dominant and commonplace.

IDENTITY

In the digital world, people experiment with identity. Some create multiple identities, different ones depending on the group or audience. In the often-disembodied online world, one is able to experiment with different ways of presenting oneself publicly. Some feel as if they can be more open and authentic online than in the face-to-face world. As one teenager explained to me, "There is the real me and the fake me. The real me is who I am when I am online, where I can more fully express myself."

Neither the search for identity nor experimenting with different ways of self-expression are new to the digital age, but we see new expressions of it now. Throughout all ages, a Christian worldview has offered a far more substantive and stable way to think about identity. Our worth and our identity come from outside of us. We are God's own, created in His image and adopted through Baptism in the name of the triune God. We are valuable because God declared us to be so, not because we have a massive following on social media. Our purpose is granted to us by God; He created us at this time and to live in this place. Our future is determined as God brings about our salvation through the work of Jesus Christ, not by any effort of our own. These persistent, unchanging truths offer distinction and certainty in a world of shifting identities, and Christians are in a position to share them.

Vocation

Similarly, human purpose is something than many today see as a creative endeavor. Some argue that purpose is something each person manufactures; it does not exist on its own. A Christian worldview, on the other hand, infuses even the most ordinary and mundane of activities with significance. This comes from our understanding of vocation. Fathers and mothers are called to love the little neighbors known as their children. The same is true for children toward their parents. We find rich meaning in the love of neighbor as citizen, in various occupations, and in many other callings as well.

Truth

Discerning what is true or false can be difficult. From realistic films and manipulated images to fake news stories and the blending of news and entertainment, it is tempting to think that truth no longer exists or that there are degrees of truth, that this is a world of rhetoric. We are inclined to believe that which is presented in the most persuasive manner rather than that which is true. We celebrate social and political commentary that appears in 140 characters and on bumper stickers. We grow disinterested in following more lengthy explanations. We turn to ad hominem attacks on those with whom we disagree instead of respectfully debating the issues. We value news as much for its entertainment value as for its accuracy and information. If we are not careful, such practices breed skepticism about truth.

Living in such a world, we begin to wonder if anything we see and hear is actually true. We join Pilate in lamenting, "What is truth?" (John 18:38), yet we abandon the search without discovering an answer. Some are content questioning, challenging, and doubting. We deconstruct and tear ideas apart, but we do not necessarily find ourselves obligated to replace them with something better or more lasting. The risk is that we will soon find ourselves living in a garbage dump of ideas that we doubt and debunk, but with a nagging longing for something that is true and real.

As Christians, we have the distinct honor and the responsibility of pointing people to that something. Jesus reminds us that He is "the way, and the truth, and the life." (John 14:6). The search for truth is not hopeless in Jesus Christ. He is real, stable, and lasting. Jesus says, "Heaven and earth will pass away, but My words will not pass away" (Matthew 24:35). This may not always be a welcome message to those immersed in the smoke and mirrors of this age, but it is a fundamental human need to have the stability and truth that only comes in Jesus Christ.

And as we remember that there is indeed truth, we also remember that there is good and evil, right and wrong, truth and lies. There is a foundation upon which to make claims and judgment about the many moral challenges of this age. This foundation is not just a matter of preference or convenience. It is God's inerrant Word, our guide and rule—just as relevant to the dilemmas of this age as it was to the dilemmas of first-century Christians.

Into the Fray

As Christians, we have the privilege of representing the unchanging truths of God's Word. We need not look any further than the Scriptures to offer people an alternative to the competing and shifting beliefs and values of this age. The short list of examples in this chapter is only a beginning, representing some of the themes that have significance when contrasted with the values of this age, a starting point for discussion and prayerful consideration. Your own list will expand as you grapple with what it means to live as a Christian in the contemporary world.

Even as we strive to represent these truths in the world at large, there are reminders to represent them within the Church. It is easy to fall prey to the spirit of the age; it resonates with our contemporary sensibilities. We find ourselves so immersed in the values of the digital age that they begin to seem natural and obvious in the current way of thinking. Yet, they are not necessarily consistent with the Scriptures and our calling to "not be conformed to this world" (Romans 12:2). We return to the Word and Sacrament as the source of renewal and strength that is central to cultivating a distinctly Christian worldview.

There was a time in world history when some Christians found it sensible and even biblically defensible to treat other people as property—namely, when some accepted and practiced slavery, perhaps because it had become commonplace, and built entire economic and social systems to depend upon it. That was undeniably a moral blind spot for generations. Although we no longer live in such a system, we are still human. What are our moral blind spots in this digital age? The fact is that 150 years ago, not all Christians embraced or condoned slavery—not all conformed to the spirit of the age. It is my prayer that you join me in humbly seeking God's grace, mercy, and wisdom for ourselves in this present age. Join me in asking God to forgive us for and heal us from our moral blind spots, and to grant us the wisdom to discern what is good and right. "Finally, brothers, whatever is true, whatever is honorable, whatever is just, whatever is pure, whatever is lovely, whatever is commendable, if there is any excellence, if there is anything worthy of praise, think about these things" (Philippians 4:8).

DIRECT ENGAGEMENT IN THE DIGITAL WORLD

The previous two approaches to engaging the digital world are largely review of earlier sections in this book. This third one is almost entirely new. It involves equipping ourselves and others to stand firm in the faith. It clarifies what God's Word says about faith and life in these current contexts. Yet, it also seeks to set up camp in the digital world. It is an effort to use the digital tools, spaces, and places to be a witness, whether explicitly or a bit more subtly.

If millions are spending an increasing amount of their lives in the digital world and immersed in digital culture, and if Christians are either silent, unrecognizable, or absent from that world, then where will others learn about Jesus? How can we be salt and light, not only in the physical world in which we live, but also in the digital ones?

Not every Christian should create a podcast, a blog, a YouTube channel, and a Pinterest account to share Bible verses, talk about Jesus, and be a voice for the Christian worldview in our culture. Some are drawn to such efforts; some even do this full-time. I am suggesting, however, that we should at least consider what role we will or will not play individually, in our families, and in our churches. There are countless ways to engage in such areas, and I encourage people to think about this with their pastors and other church members. In the end, you may decide this is not a priority, but I offer it for your consideration because people online need to hear from Christians. What follows is just a short list of possibilities of how you can be a witness in the digital world, although there are hundreds of others as well. Please do not feel limited by what I share. Use this list as a starting point, but consider gathering with others in your church to come up with more possibilities.

The Church Website

While many churches use social media to connect with current members, prospective members, and others in the community, the idea of a dedicated website is still relevant. Content is king in much of the digital world, and if your website has quality content, it will show up when people search certain keywords. I encourage congregations to explore sharing as much as they are willing and able on the web. Church websites can include information about the congregation's history, contact information, directions, church groups and activities and when those activities occur, and the times and days of worship services.

In addition, any of the congregation's Bible studies should be mentioned on the site. Although copyright protected documents cannot be shared, written reflections by the pastor or other Bible study leaders can be regular features. Perhaps leaders and participants in action could also be shared.

The web is friendly to stories and images, so the more you communicate in those formats, the better your chance of people finding your content. In this information-rich world, why not join in contributing good and positive content to that mix?

A little book by Austin Kleon called *Show Your Work!* points out a basic truth about the nature of living in our connected age. If there is no information about you online, to those who are searching online, it is as if you do not exist.[68] You *do* exist, of course, but how will people know that? I argue that an important part of connecting with prospective members and people in the community is taking time to make the stories and activities of our churches visible and discoverable. This extends beyond static content like the church mission statement—tell people more about who you are and what you do. Encourage church members who have the gift of writing to write stories about what is taking place at your church. Ask individuals who are interested in photography and videography to provide visuals to accompany the stories. This does not need to be a complicated, time-consuming task, but it can be a meaningful one.

Once we start to build a collection of stories, images, and the like, church members can share them on social media, inviting friends, colleagues, and family members to join in the activity. Since so much communication today is happening in this format, we can help spread the message by making it understandable and sharable. It does not take much to add a hyperlink to articles, images, and events that make it easy for people to share it on their favorite social media outlets with a single click.

This does not mean that we should post anything and everything online. For exam-

---

68   Austin Kleon, *Show Your Work!* (New York: Workman Publishing, 2014).

ple, we do not post images of people without their consent. We need to create simple guidelines for who can post and how, whether to attach names to images, and more. This might seem burdensome, but it is the ethical and safe way to go.

Before we move on to other ideas, I want to share a story that speaks to the potential of simply being available online. In the 1990s, I served as a director of outreach for a church, and I helped build the first church website. In addition to basic content, we created a simple page called "Ask the Pastor" and invited anyone visiting the page to submit a question to the pastor. Questions could be about practical matters, like meeting times and the nature of certain events, or they could be theological or doctrinal questions.

Not long after creating the page, a woman filled out the form. She had a history of going to churches that might be appropriately labeled as Christian cults or highly controlling and manipulative churches, ones that discouraged communication with nonmembers and used guilt to drive compliance and conformity. Despite these experiences, this woman still sought a church home, one free from such tactics. What started as one question submitted online became a conversation that eventually led to an in-person meeting with the pastor. In the end, she did not join the congregation, but this simple encounter reinforced for me the value of simply inviting people to reach out.

SOCIAL MEDIA PRESENCE

Social media sites come and go. Some last for years, while others are around for only a short time. A social media site is any site (or mobile application) that allows the sharing of information, ideas, and interests. It includes text, pictures, video, or a combination of these. Social media also gives the option of following other people. Some limit how much text can be shared, the size of the images, or the length of the videos. Many churches are turning to social media to share news and information, sometimes even more information than what is on their main websites. Still others use social media sites as their primary online presence.

Of course, this is not just about a church being present on social media; it is also about individuals making use of the technology. Each of us makes decisions about which social media to use (if any). Most people have one or two preferred sites. Yet, this is a place where people share news, discuss that news, and share images and text about their lives. It is a place where many of us connect with family, friends, and colleagues. While some find social media to be a distraction and avoid it at all costs, others find it to be a way to learn, connect, and encourage.

PODCASTS

Anyone with a little bit of inexpensive equipment is able to create his or her own audio or video podcast. A podcast is really just an audio or video file that people can download to their computer or mobile device. They are typically in a series of episodes, and listeners or viewers can subscribe so they're notified when the latest podcast becomes available. They can range from solo podcasts where an individual talks about a topic of personal interest or experience (and hopefully of interest to an audience) to full shows with multiple hosts, interviews, and advertisements. Some pastors turn their sermons into podcasts, making them available for anyone to download and listen to.

There are podcasts on almost every imaginable topic: conspiracy theories, sports, gaming, cooking, starting a new business, the future, literature, comedy, education, politics, new technology, parenting, dating, and spirituality. There are even podcasts about podcasts. While some podcasts garner the attention of only a small group of listeners, others reach as wide an audience as some nationally broadcast radio and television shows. Unlike radio and television shows, creating a podcast has little or no cost.

While not everyone will be inspired to create a podcast, their widespread use is a promising opportunity for Christian witness. There are many podcasts on Christian topics, but there is opportunity for Christians to offer a witness through podcasts about any topic.

BLOGS

A blog is a website that organizes your posts or articles by the day and time in which they are published. Again, there are blogs about almost any topic imaginable. Like podcasts, they are free or inexpensive to start. Some sites charge a fee to host the blog, but there is a long list of reputable options for anyone with the desire and time to create his or her own blog.

There is already a strong presence of Christian bloggers on countless topics and vocations, and some have garnered a large enough following that it is a full-time job. Some sell advertisement space on their site to generate revenue (which is, then, income). Others create and sell products, such as books, mugs, and T-shirts. Some direct visitors to products on retail sites like Amazon.com, which pay the blogger a small commission for each sale. Many others do not do any of that, but blog instead for the sheer satisfaction of communicating and sharing ideas.

FREELANCE WRITING

Blogging is not the only way to share writing online. Countless blogs, online magazines, and news sites welcome editorials and articles, and some of the major outlets get hundreds of thousands or even millions of viewers a day. People with a perspective submit their ideas to these sites, and sometimes they get published. If the digital age is indeed a central marketplace of ideas, then we desperately need Christians who are willing to engage the larger secular world through their writing abilities. Some churches even host formal writing groups to encourage this and other forms of writing, but individuals with the will can do it as well.

Contributing to blogs and other online media involves identifying a site you like, reaching out or pitching your idea, or submitting a draft for consideration. Those who choose to do this need to prepare for some rejections. That is just part of the process; do not be discouraged. Whenever possible, seek feedback and learn from each submission and response, but I encourage you to persist.

While the individual or the local congregation can create Christian news sites and blogs where others share their stories and ideas, there is also something promising about writing and publishing on sites that have an existing readership. In addition, some of these sites have a diverse audience, allowing us to communicate our message and the Gospel more broadly.

DIGITAL STORYTELLING AND VIDEO SHARING

There continues to be a trend toward video in the digital world. (However, text-based communication is not slowing down.) As of 2016, YouTube was ranked by some as the second largest search engine on the Internet.[69] If you want to communicate a message, especially one that people are likely to share with others, video is a compelling option. It sticks out amid other text-heavy messages. It allows you to communicate emotion and other nuances effectively. It is also shown to be effective in building rapport with viewers.

While professionally produced videos can be expensive, those are not the only videos people watch online. The democratization of knowledge creation and sharing we examined in chapter 10 manifests itself in video as well. Do not underestimate the impact of authentic yet substantive videos created by amateurs. In an age when some filmmakers win awards with little more equipment than a cell phone, this is not out of reach for you or anyone else.

I do not want to minimize the value of professional filmmakers and videographers. Like any trained, experienced professional, they are skilled at communicating a mes-

---

69   Tony Edward, "YouTube Ranking Factors: Getting Ranked in the Second Largest Search Engine," Search Engine Land, July 24, 2015, http://searchengineland.com/youtube-ranking-factors-getting-ranked-second-largest-search-engine-225533 (accessed March 19, 2017).

sage effectively. Consideration should be given to the type of video needed, the intended message, and the desired outcome. That is, there is rationale for investing in and collaborating with a professional videographer. At the same time, individuals, churches, and schools looking to share an impromptu or informal message need not wait for that type of funding to be in place.

In the late 1990s, digital storytelling emerged as a trend. Digital storytelling is the modern form of the ancient art of storytelling, using modern digital tools of audio and video. It emerged as a powerful way for people to tell stories about themselves, their families, their communities, and more. Instead of a talking head on the screen, digital stories usually include an audio narration of the story, a series of images or video clips to help illustrate the story, and appropriate background music. It might help to think of the Ken Burns style of documentary that many recognize as award-winning, only not as polished.

I led a few digital storytelling workshops in the early 2000s. People came with their ideas and collections of images, and over a couple of days, they produced digital narratives. We started by sharing our stories, giving one another feedback, and revising the projects. People came with stories about their faith, family, community, even beloved pets. From there, we used basic equipment to capture a quality audio recording of each person narrating his or her story.

After that, we reviewed the photographs people brought with them. While it does not always work in a condensed workshop time frame, sometimes people take photos after they write their script, brainstorming images that will best communicate different aspects of the narrative, and then they intentionally seek out and capture those images. Either way, I walked people through how to use one of several software products that let you to combine an audio narration with images. Today, simple apps like GarageBand are all a person needs to create a video.

Finally, we considered background music we could add to help enhance the message (making sure the students adhered to any copyright laws, of course). Sometimes leaving the music out is the best option. Other times, the right music helps tell the story. Again, adding this component to the video is something anyone can learn in a few minutes.

Once they finished creating their digital stories, they shared them with one another, offering encouragement and candid feedback. In only one weekend, people walked away with compelling videos they could post online and share with friends and family.

This is not out of reach for anyone. People can create and share family stories. A congregation could host a digital storytelling event, giving members a chance to share stories of the faith. Then, if they choose, they can add their content to the ever-growing world of online video, making it possible for others to benefit from their stories.

I once talked to a woman who told me about her son who went through what she called a "prodigal son" phase. She described the fear and pain she felt during this time. Many people in her church, including her pastor, shared encouraging words, prayed with and for her; some told their own stories of working through challenges with prodigal sons and daughters. In time, as with the original prodigal son, her son returned home and to the Church. Overjoyed and wanting to offer encouragement to other families experiencing similar challenges, she explored the idea of creating a collection of prodigal son digital stories as a source of hope. I do not know if she followed through, but this and many other possibilities await our embrace. I get excited when I imagine the possibilities as individuals and groups in congregations explore how they can be creators and storytellers in this way. Yes, there are billions of hours of video online, but if YouTube is one of the top search engines on the web, and people in their times of trial search for just the right term, your future video might be just what they need.

This does not necessarily need to be a formal digital story. Others create and share short and informal videos of all sorts. Any of these have the potential to bless and benefit others. Some might only receive a dozen views, but those twelve people will have watched something that shares the important message of hope. Why not share videos that give us an opportunity to witness to the promises of our Savior?

Visuals and Infographics

The visual medium continues to gain traction as many people are introduced to an idea through still images, cartoons, videos, and other forms of multimedia. Videos and images often go viral online, garnering hundreds of thousands or millions of views from around the world. This is a valuable means of connecting with people about matters of faith as well.

When we trace the history of art in Christianity, we learn that stained glass windows in beautiful cathedrals and churches of past centuries offered a celebration of aesthetic beauty, but also served a more basic function. These stained glass windows communicated biblical narratives to people, some of whom did not know how to read. Preachers expounded upon what parishioners saw in these windows, offering greater detail to the narratives, but the images still played an important role. I see visuals as having a similar role today. If we want to engage people in the world about important matters of faith, the visual element of the digital world is a promising way to start such conversations.

Participating in Online Communities

Many Christians explain that their engagement in the local community allows them to love their neighbors through the calling of citizen. They build authentic and meaningful relationships with others. They also find that opportunities arise for them to be a more direct Christian witness as they build those relationships. Peter reminds us of an important lesson: "But in your hearts honor Christ the Lord as holy, always being prepared to make a defense to anyone who asks you for a reason for the hope that is in you; yet do it with gentleness and respect" (1 Peter 3:15).

People do not gather only at the local coffee shop, barbershop, marketplace, or American Legion today. They also gather and connect in online communities, as we have already explored. These are opportunities for us as Christians to connect with others in mutually beneficial ways. We explore what it means to love our neighbors in online communities. We also put ourselves in positions where opportunities might arise for us to be witnesses or to be a blessing to people in need.

There are many online communities that explore any imaginable interest or topic. I am not arguing that every Christian should join such communities, but many are already doing so. For those people, I simply encourage them to consider what it means to love their neighbors in these communities and to be Christian witnesses when and if opportunities present themselves.

This concept might be new to some readers, but perhaps they are interested in and open to exploring the possibilities. For those readers, I suggest starting with personal activities and interests. Are you a teacher? There are countless educator communities on many topics and subtopics. Are you interested in cooking, carpentry, great novels, films, video games, entrepreneurship, travel, fitness, or something else? Why not begin by browsing the communities that exist and trying them out? As we go about living out our vocations and discovering what it means to live in an increasingly digital world, we find ourselves building new connections and relationships. It is within these connections and relationships that we also discover new neighbors to love and new ways to love existing neighbors.

Creating and Leading an Online Community

Exploring the existing communities made possible by digital tools and contexts is a valuable way to build new relationships and connections, but these tools also provide opportunity to start new communities. They allow us the flexibility to create a group around a personal interest or need, to shape the group from the outset, and to take a direct leadership role in the group.

Because technologies change every day, specific tools or technologies I mention will become dated soon after publication of this book. For the sake of illustration, however, I offer three simple examples that can be easily replaced with other technology options available. Facebook, a massive online social network, makes it easy for anyone to create a public or private group around a topic of interest. LinkedIn, a social network focused on professional connections and interests, also allows members to create groups and communities around shared needs or interests. Similarly, Google offers a service called Google Groups, which allows people to engage in communication through online forums or email-based groups. These are only three of literally thousands of options available today.

There are endless reasons for creating an online community. It might be a group of Christian business people who want to build online support and encourage one another in modeling Christian ethics in the workplace. It could be a group of people going through a shared struggle. It might be an online book club that forms to read and discuss various texts. It might be a network of pastors or church workers working toward a common goal who can benefit from sharing ideas and resources. It could be online Bible study communities for those whose work and life situations make it challenging to participate in the face-to-face equivalent. Amid the many options, what matters is that the group has a clear purpose that resonates with a critical mass of people at the beginning.

Groups can be open (welcoming anyone to join) or closed (limiting participation to select people). The status is determined by what is best for the intended purpose and goals of the group. Private groups allow people to feel more comfortable sharing freely. They also allow for the group creator or moderators to more carefully decide whether a given person is suited for the group. Some conversations do not apply to everyone. Open groups, on the other hand, make it easier to grow, reach more people, and invite others to join. Each option has its benefits and limitations.

The digital world represents a common means by which people connect and communicate. While we are wise to be careful about letting it undermine our value for and commitment to off-line communities and relationships, we recognize that this is where many people spend their time today. As such, this is an opportunity to meet people where they are.

For those who choose to create their own communities, I offer a few important suggestions. First, just creating a community does not mean that people will join it or be interested. It takes time, persistence, and effort to build and nurture a vibrant community. It is helpful to find others who created successful communities and seek their advice. Learn from them what worked and what did not work. Second, as with face-to-face communities, it is helpful to establish and communicate shared goals and agreed upon rules and expectations. Third, this is an organic process; it is not a perfect science. So, I encourage people to consider this process to be a shared experiment and a constant work in progress. Recognize when things are not working, get feedback from the group, make adjustments, monitor those adjustments, and go from there. Finally, remember that God's Word applies in the digital world as much as it does in the physical world. Seek wisdom from the Bible as you consider how to shape and influence the community. This includes how to treat one another, address conflict, pursue truth, focus on love of neighbor, and recognize the Scriptures as the inerrant, infallible, inspired Word of God—the norm and source of the doctrines that inform our lives, thoughts, and actions.

CURATING RESOURCES

When someone seeks information, people, or resources online, a common place to start is a dominant search engine like Google. According to one source, there were over 3.5 billion people on the Internet by the end of 2016.[70] There are also more than a billion websites on the Internet.[71] This takes the needle in a haystack cliché to a completely different level. Because of this, many people turn to trusted people, groups, and online sources to provide them with suggestions and curated resources when they need information. A trusted blogger shared the top ten most important books about a topic that interests you, so you order a few of those books and read them. Someone you follow on social media tests recipes and shares the results, so you try one that turned out well. Another person on social media shares a list of the top best college options, influencing what you or a friend consider for your own children. This type of sharing is an important part of how people find information today.

Sharing online is a form of endorsement. What we share represents our beliefs, values, and priorities. For example, we find ample instances of parents giving advice to one another about which films are appropriate or inappropriate for children of various

---

70 "World Internet Users Statistics and 2017 World Population Stats," Internet World Stats, http://www.internetworldstats.com/stats.htm (accessed March 19, 2017).

71 "Total Number of Websites," Internet Live Stats, http://www.internetlivestats.com/total-number-of-websites/ (accessed March 19, 2017).

ages. Other recommendations are related to products and services. Amid such sharing we have the opportunity to embody our Christian beliefs and values, to love our neighbors, and to witness our faith in Jesus as Lord and Savior. Sharing ideas and resources is a simple but significant way to be a positive influence in the digital world.

Online Identity Management

How we represent ourselves online communicates something to others. The pictures we post on social media express something about our interests, beliefs, and values. The same thing is true with political commentary, how we agree and disagree with others, and what we share about ourselves. Each comment we make, each image we share, each resource we recommend, each message we communicate in the digital world might end up being seen by a lot of people.

God's Word is far from silent on such matters. In 1 Corinthians 8, Paul gives advice to Christians in Corinth regarding a contemporary challenge. In Corinth, some of the meat available for purchase was previously sacrificed to gods in the temples. There was debate about whether Christians should purchase or even eat such meat. Is eating the meat an expression of support for these false religions and their associated beliefs? In chapter 8, Paul explains that the meat, regardless whether it was sacrificed to idols, is just food. These idols do not actually exist.

Although Paul argues that there is nothing morally wrong with eating that meat, he points to another important consideration, one rooted in the call to love our neighbors. In 1 Corinthians 8:9–10, he explains it this way: "But take care that this right of yours does not somehow become a stumbling block to the weak. For if anyone sees you who have knowledge eating in an idol's temple, will he not be encouraged, if his conscience is weak, to eat food offered to idols?" In other words, there are times when we choose not to act upon our Christian freedom for the sake of another person. We do not act or speak in ways that cause others to sin or to question the Christian faith.

I remember struggling with this as a teenager. My stepfather insisted that I wear my best clothes to church. This, he explained, is an act of respect, showing that the weekly time of worship is no mundane or ordinary experience. I am a participant in the Divine Service when I go to church. I did not disagree with the spirit of what he communicated, but we differed on which of my clothes were best. I argued that my blue jeans, which cost more than my dress pants, were my best clothing. I did not think that a sport coat and tie represented my best.

We have nothing in Scripture to inform who was right on this matter, but there are two teachings from the Bible that made the debate a moot point. First, the Scriptures are abundantly clear on my calling to honor my father and mother (Exodus 20:12). Second, in 1 Corinthians 8:8–13, we read about the dangers of being a stumbling block. Even if I was convinced that, in my Christian freedom, it was acceptable for me to wear blue jeans to church, my clothing choice was not my only consideration. I knew that others in church did not agree with me and that my decision to wear jeans could be a stumbling block for some, if not at least a distraction. As such, it was clear to me that the best decision was to wear a sport coat and tie to church.

In 1 Corinthians 10:23, Paul further explained that "'all things are lawful,' but not all things are helpful. 'All things are lawful,' but not all things build up." These words apply as much to how we manage our online identity as they do to eating food sacrificed to idols or wardrobe choices for Sunday morning worship. Online expression is not simply expressing ourselves. As Christians, everything we do is also fundamentally an expression of our love for God and for neighbor.

Online Volunteering

Because many people spend much of their time online, there are ample service and volunteering opportunities in the digital world. We can engage in online tutoring for struggling students. We can serve as guest presenters in classrooms, doing so remotely using video conferencing tools. We can participate in the online equivalent of pen pal programs (sometimes called key pal programs). We can write letters of encouragement. Online funding websites allow us to offer direct financial support to people and organizations, including offering small loans to people in other parts of the world, helping them to start businesses that serve their communities and support their families. We can write for a nonprofit or faith-based organization, helping spread the word on an important issue, upcoming event, or new need. Or we can design or manage a website or an online community like we discussed previously.

As I have sometimes playfully explained, we live in this strange age where it is indeed possible to change the world in your pajamas. More specifically, since the digital world consists of our many neighbors in the world, there are ways to love them through this developing idea of virtual volunteerism. This need not replace other efforts, but it is certainly an opportunity worth our consideration today.

Starting Digital Ethnography Teams

The ideas listed in the previous pages are specific ways in which individuals and groups can be involved and directly engaged in the digital world. There are countless other options as well. However, I offer one last idea for your consideration. It is not as common, but given the ideas discussed in this book, I contend that it could be a blessing to those involved as well as many others. It is what I refer to as digital ethnography teams.

Ethnography is a form of research that usually employs methods such as observation, participant observation, interviews, and the study of artifacts to understand people, cultures, and communities. As an academic, I consider ethnography to be an important aspect of my own research, and I have significant formal training in conducting research with this method. However, one does not necessarily need countless graduate classes to learn from observation and interviews. With time, practice, and instruction, any of us can learn to do this, at least in small ways.

What does this have to do with the digital world? Throughout this book, I have been building a case that the digital world is about so much more than technology. It is about people. It is about beliefs and values. It is about questions of what it means to be human, the nature of relationships, purpose, and much more. Yet, many of us live in this digital world in largely unexamined ways. We rarely stop to consider why we are using technology and how it influences our own beliefs and values and those of our communities, families, churches, and workplaces.

I offered caution about jumping to overly judgmental or legalistic claims about the digital world, as well as the opposite extreme of blindly accepting and embracing every new development or innovation. A third reaction to our ever-changing digital world is one of prayerful consideration with our Bibles open. This mind-set requires an exploration of the affordances and limitations to better understand how technology and different aspects of the digital world shape us.

For that, I offer this last suggestion of building teams of people in our churches who demonstrate an interest in examining some of these matters directly and sharing their findings with others in the community. I call these digital ethnography teams: groups of people who are willing to study and analyze what is going on in the digital world, examine the Scriptures with these trends in mind, and host substantive conversations with others in the community about what they discover.

This is a great way to demonstrate that we want to listen and learn from others in this emerging digital landscape. We observe. When appropriate, we participate and take careful notes as we do so. We interview people about their experiences. We read relevant books and other resources that might guide our learning and discovery. Then, we use all of this to promote more informed conversations about faith and life in the digital world.

This intentional approach helps us grow in understanding and make wise decisions about what to do next. Again, I caution against ending up with a definitive list of what people should do and not do to avoid falling into the trap of legalism. Yet, having listened and learned, we will be in a much better position to prayerfully consider how the unchanging truths of God's Word do indeed apply to life today—and how we can heed the wisdom of the Scriptures in making decisions about our and our families' participation in the digital world.

DISCUSSION AND REFLECTION QUESTIONS

- Among the three main approaches to faith and life in the digital world, which one do you do the most: relate to people, prepare for battle, or engage directly?

- In *Peace Child*, the missionary discovered something within the culture of the people that he could use as a starting point for sharing the Gospel. Try to identify one or two "Peace Child" analogies or illustrations that might help you communicate important biblical truths to people in the digital world.

- In the section on preparing for battle, we reviewed a number of important ideas about where God's Word has special relevance for people in the digital world. Which do you see as having the greatest importance in your own life, family, school, church, and community? Why?

- What other ideas would you add to the list in the preparing for battle section? Are there other themes or trends in the digital world that you think call for us to share a contrasting Christian worldview?

- In the list of ideas for direct engagement in the digital world, which are you already doing or considering? Why? What help might you need in order to take action in one or more of these areas? Who or what might be able to provide that help?

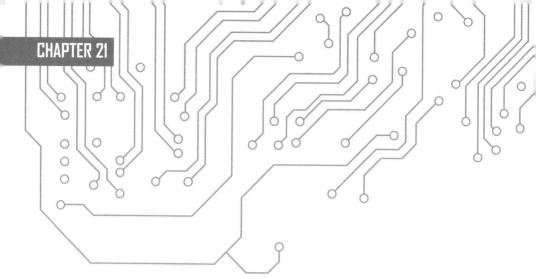

CHAPTER 21

Dis-integrating Technology

Imagine being a high school freshman on the football team. You prepare all summer, go to tryouts, and are delighted that you make the cut. You are on the team! At your first team meeting, the coach draws everyone together for the opening pep talk and says something like, "Welcome to the team. We are going to be an extraordinary group of people this year. As a top priority, I have decided that we are going to be the most high-tech team in our state, maybe even in the nation. We are going to integrate technology into our practices, our coaching methods, your physical training, and our games." If the football example does not work for you, consider two parents sitting their children down and giving a similar pep talk. "We are going to be the most high-tech family in our neighborhood."

You are unlikely to find many teams or families that talk like this because integrating technology is not the priority for a football team or family. We use technology when it meets a need or goal, but it would be hard to find examples of people who consider integrating technology to be a wise or commendable focus in these areas.

Oddly enough, I have seen communities with such a focus. In education, especially in the late 1990s, there was a strong push for integrating technology into the classroom. Some schools spent large sums of money on computer hardware and software without any clear goal or rationale beyond "integrating technology." There was a near obsession with becoming cutting-edge, but when asked about the educational goals or philosophy behind it, many struggled to answer. Technology use became an end more than a means.

It can be difficult to see the ways in which technology shapes us and our communities when it is integrated into so many aspects of our everyday lives. This is not that different from recognizing our own accents. For a sabbatical, my family and I moved from Wisconsin to Connecticut for a semester. When someone commented on my accent, I became confused. I do not have an accent—or so I thought. Of course, they were right. But my patterns of speech were so integrated and familiar that it was difficult for me to recognize them. The same is true with thoughts and habits influenced by the digital world. They become so familiar and commonplace that we lose the ability to recognize technology's role and influence in our lives. That is why, as much as I advocate for using technology in positive ways, I also encourage people to consider what I call dis-integrating technology.

Some talk about technology diets, unplugging, or digital detox for days or weeks. Doing so gives them perspective. A temporary distance from certain technologies allows people to revisit the role and influence of technology in their lives. Others do it to reduce the stress that often comes with information overload. In addition, others find it to be a helpful exercise in reevaluating goals and priorities, and then considering the extent to which technology helps or hinders those goals. Still others use this technique to focus on things that get less attention when they are fully immersed in a technology-rich lifestyle.

Some people assume that a digital detox requires some major and extended time commitment. While that is a possibility, it is not the only option. Some find it helpful to set aside an hour per day, a day, a week, or one weekend a year. Still others might opt for more extended separation from certain practices, but not others. Or it could be the decision to experiment with decreasing a certain type of technology use for a few weeks or months to understand its role and influence in a person's life. Consider some of these options:

- Turn off phone notifications and alerts to avoid frequent interruptions throughout the day. Instead, dedicate certain times of day to checking email and other messages.

- Replace an hour of evening media consumption with reading or some other off-line activity, perhaps soon before bed. There is some evidence that screen time interrupts sleep patterns, so this practice may allow for better sleep.

- Put the phone on airplane mode during certain days, times, and events to prevent frequent interruptions.

- Schedule an unplugged day or weekend for an individual project or a family activity.

- Download and use one of the many mobile device apps that allows you to monitor the amount and type of media use that occupies your time. Review this for a few weeks or a month, and then choose to limit your usage of certain types of technology for a short time or an extended period of time.

- Replace technology-rich time with outdoor activities such as hiking, walking, or some athletic activity to enjoy with others.

- Delete the most time-consuming app on your mobile device for one week and then reevaluate your need for it at the end of the week.

- Ask for an accountability partner at work or home to help you become more aware of technology interruptions, giving you a gentle reminder when you are distracted by technology interactions, conversations, or other online activities.

- Keep a journal of your technology usage and review it at the end of the day. Based upon what you find, set goals for the next day. Continue this for a couple of weeks to help you understand the role of technology in your life. This will also help you evaluate how technology is amplifying or muzzling other values and goals.

- Experiment with a half-day or full-day retreat where you enjoy quiet activities, identify goals, set aside time for prayer, and engage in Scripture or devotional reading. Some find it useful to do this quarterly or annually.

TIPS FOR DIS-INTEGRATING ACTIVITIES

Keep in mind that I am not suggesting these activities as some sort of pious sacrifice. These are intended to help you discover the role of technology in one or more areas of your life, to understand how technology influences you, to set goals, and to reprioritize. When we are constantly moving and not pausing, it is difficult to reflect.

There are no definitive rules on whether or how to engage in dis-integrating or detox activities, but based upon conversations with others and firsthand experience, I offer a few options. Consider the following options, but please do not be limited by them.

Have a Partner or a Group

While some of these work great as solitary activities, you may find it useful to go through this process with a partner or even a small group. Seek out someone else willing to give it a try, clarify what you will be doing, try it out, and take advantage of the chance to debrief what you are learning and experiencing along the way.

Inventory Your Technology Usage

As I mentioned, one of the ideas for a detox includes establishing a baseline. How much technology do you use now? How do you use it? Engaging in this activity in preparation for unplugging can help you clarify your goals.

Establish Goals

The previous suggestion leads us to the idea of goals. What do you want to achieve as a result of this time? Is it a chance to gain some distance and perspective on the use of technology? Is it to focus specifically upon the spiritual implications of technology in your life, family, church, workplace, or community? Is it to reflect on how technology aligns with your many vocations? Maybe you have another goal. Choosing a goal will help you focus your efforts.

Develop a Plan

What will you be doing and for how long? Do you need some accountability? Answering these questions will give you clarity about what you are going to be doing. Do not hesitate to adjust the plan if it is not helping you to achieve your goal(s).

Pick One Thing at a Time

Some people feel like unplugging must be an all or nothing endeavor—either turn everything off or do nothing. There are no rules like this. You can learn a great deal from systematically stepping away from or limiting one or two specific uses of technology for a time. Then, you might choose to move on to something else. You can experiment with this to see what is helpful.

Take Small Breaks

As with picking one thing at a time, it is sometimes useful to consider short breaks. It might be an hour, a morning, an evening, or a day. We do not always need to be thinking in terms of weeks, months, or years. You might decide to extend the time at some point, but it is often helpful to start small.

Set Aside the Self-Righteousness

This is not some good work. We are not doing this to please God or earn His favor. Jesus Christ took care of that for us on the cross. This is a chance to learn. Beware of the temptation to look down on others along the way. You might use this to decrease your binge-watching of media, allowing you to read more or engage in activities that you value. That is great. Just be careful about casting judgment on others for not choosing the same options. For the most part, we are dealing with matters that are not explicitly commanded or forbidden in Scripture. That does not mean we cannot share what we are doing and learning so others can benefit from it; we simply want to beware of the self-righteousness trap as we do.

Plan What You Will Do Instead

Just giving up media for a certain time is often not as helpful without deciding in advance what you will do with the extra time. Otherwise, it is easy to feel as if this is just about making some sort of sacrifice. You spend your time thinking about not using the technology instead of doing something you consider to be more valuable.

Journal and Debrief

The purpose of these activities is to learn from them. As such, it is useful to journal about what you are thinking and learning. When possible, talk about your experience with others; this can be helpful in the learning process as well. What replaced your time? What changed? What stayed the same? Did this exercise give you any new insights into your use of different technologies and how that aligns with your beliefs and values? Is there anything you want to try next or do differently because of this experiment?

CONCLUDING THOUGHTS

Technology is certainly integrated into our lives, but as I illustrated in the opening paragraphs of this chapter, few of us believe that simply integrating technology into our lives is the ultimate goal. At the same time, technology has a way of becoming second nature and so integrated that it is difficult to reflect on its use in our lives. We have goals, values, and fundamental beliefs that are far more important to us than the technology in our lives, and dis-integrating activities might be useful as we try to find the right balance and be more deliberate in our use of technology. I am not suggesting some rule or set of regulations in this chapter. Simply consider this an invitation to experiment, explore the possibilities, and join in learning more about faith and life in a digital age.

DISCUSSION AND REFLECTION QUESTIONS

- How do you currently create the distance that allows you to be thoughtful about the role of technology in your life, family, work, school, community, or elsewhere?

- Which of the ideas in this chapter would you like to try and why? Is there anything holding you back? What will it take for you to move forward?

- Are there other ideas not mentioned in this chapter that you want to try or would encourage others to try when it comes to dis-integrating, unplugging, or detoxing? If you had to choose one or two key ideas that you most want to remember or talk about from this chapter, what would they be? Why those?

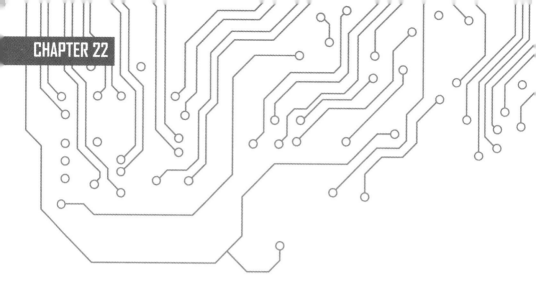

CHAPTER 22

Keeping First Things First

We live in fascinating times. Innovations and technological advancements continue to create new ways to think, work, communicate, and so much more. From medical innovations to the information revolution, many of us look at these advancements with gratitude. We thank God for them as blessings.

As I offer concluding thoughts in this brief final chapter, I hope and pray that you join me in recognizing that these are fascinating but complex times. Just as a technology has benefits, it also has limitations and challenges. There are many opportunities to use technologies to love our neighbors, but there are also countless ways they can isolate us, either stopping us from interacting with the neighbors we are called to love or allowing us to become so inwardly focused that we lose sight of others' needs. To that end, we prayerfully consider what it means to live as Christians in the digital world today. There are opportunities and there are challenges.

The rate of technological innovation is increasing exponentially, which makes it even more important to ground ourselves in that which does not change: God's love for us in Christ. This perfect love is a constant; it is something upon which we can depend, even as the virtual aspects of our world are in constant flux. His love is the anchor in our lives, families, and churches, and it remains of paramount importance throughout all time. If it seems that I have repeated that message throughout this book, then you would be correct. Out of everything written in this book, that fundamental truth is the most important point. Without it, we find ourselves adrift, uncertain of where we are going, lacking a sense of direction, and grappling with the fears and anxieties that can so easily consume us in a world out of our control and operating at an increasingly frenzied pace. With it, we stay anchored, even amid some of the most fluid and unpredictable changes in our world.

Earlier in the book, I shared the story of my father's death and how I vividly recall my thoughts the night he died many years ago. Almost everything in my life was about to change, and even the things that did not change instantly became less stable and predictable. Even if we prioritize the people in our lives as more important than the demands technology wants to put on us, none of us has a guarantee that the people in our lives today will be the people in our lives tomorrow. Even when we prioritize people over technology, they still cannot fill us. They will still let us down, because they are still human. There is, however, one unchanging person in our lives. Our heavenly Father is unchanging. His love for us in Jesus Christ is constant and unchanging. His promises are unchanging. His Word is a constant and reliable norm and source of truth in our lives. Our greatest needs are met only in relationship with this unchanging God of grace and mercy.

Over the years, I have had the opportunity to speak with many young people who experience extreme distress over relationships with other people. Friendships become strained. Bullies come and go. Fears and anxieties about what others think seem almost unbearable at times. Some of these events are only amplified by the technologies through which we communicate. The challenges are not just for young people, of course. I meet many adults who are overwhelmed by the workplace demands of 24/7 contact through technology. Others experience anxiety about whether their jobs will be replaced by technology. And others stress over the constant technological changes that call for learning and relearning new tasks, skills, and technologies. Nothing in the technological world seems to stay the same long enough for us to become comfortable with it. Or just as we get comfortable, something replaces what was new a few moments ago. For Christians, the message of what is unchanging—God's love in Christ—is a rich and healing source of comfort and strength. It might not take away the struggles of the present, but it gives us perspective for today and tomorrow. We are better able to handle these struggles when we remember that the most important things in life are not in flux. God is in control. His love is unfailing.

Here is commonly shared analogy about priorities in life: Imagine a man's life was represented by a large, empty jar. This man loved the pleasures of his life, and so he made them a priority. He poured a large bag of pebbles into his empty jar to represent those pleasures, and a fourth of his jar is filled. After his pleasures, the man then attended to the needs of his work. So, he added some larger rocks to the jar. Then, the man attended to the needs of close friends, who were represented by even larger rocks. Next came the priority of family, represented by very large rocks. Those, too, went into the jar. Finally, there was the priority of the man's faith in Jesus Christ, the largest rock of all. But when the man went to put this rock into his jar, there was no room. The jar was already full of pebbles and other rocks; the man had left no room in his life for his faith.

No analogy is perfect. Faith is not a quantifiable thing, unlike the rocks in this story. The faith of a child is just as real and salvific as that of a missionary who spends decades sharing the message of Jesus Christ in the harshest of circumstances. Faith is a gift of God, brought about by the Holy Spirit through Word and Sacrament. Yet, this jar analogy helps us picture the nature of life in an increasingly digital world.

Much of what you have read in this book is little more than an invitation to reverse the order of putting those stones in the jar. What happens if we start with what is most important instead of filling our lives first with the technologies and other distractions that can so easily occupy our time? Then, with the most important thing already in place, we can explore the proper role of the many technologies that come and go in our lives.

Again, we do not get to choose the age in which we live, but we can decide how we respond to that age. How will you respond in this digital age? How will you challenge yourself and others to think more deeply and deliberately about the ways technologies shape your beliefs and values? How do we learn to use technology in ways that amplify our deepest-held beliefs and values rather than muzzle them? How can we equip ourselves to thrive in this digital world while being faithful to the Scriptures? How might we learn to love our neighbors in this digital world? These are a few of the many questions we have explored in this book. I invite you to join me in continuing this exploration.

DISCUSSION AND REFLECTION QUESTIONS

- After reading this book, how has your view of the digital world changed? Explain.

- What practices do you find helpful as you work toward the goal of making room in your life for your most important priorities?

- Now that you are at the end of this book, what is next for you? What do you want to do with what you have learned?